Writing the Critical Essay

Web 2.0

An OPPOSING VIEWPOINTS® Guide

Lauri S. Friedman, *Book Editor*

OPPOSING
VIEWPOINTS®
SERIES

GREENHAVEN PRESS
A part of Gale, Cengage Learning

GALE
CENGAGE Learning™

Detroit • New York • San Francisco • New Haven, Conn • Waterville, Maine • London

GALE
CENGAGE Learning

Christine Nasso, *Publisher*
Elizabeth Des Chenes, *Managing Editor*

© 2011 Greenhaven Press, a part of Gale, Cengage Learning

Gale and Greenhaven Press are registered trademarks used herein under license.

For more information, contact:
Greenhaven Press
27500 Drake Rd.
Farmington Hills, MI 48331-3535
Or you can visit our Internet site at gale.cengage.com

For product information and technology assistance, contact us at

Gale Customer Support, 1-800-877-4253
For permission to use material from this text or product, submit all requests online at www.cengage.com/permissions

Further permissions questions can be e-mailed to permissionrequest@cengage.com

Articles in Greenhaven Press anthologies are often edited for length to meet page requirements. In addition, original titles of these works are changed to clearly present the main thesis and to explicitly indicate the author's opinion. Every effort is made to ensure that Greenhaven Press accurately reflects the original intent of the authors. Every effort has been made to trace the owners of copyrighted material.

Cover image © Deanne Fitzmaurice/Corbis

LIBRARY OF CONGRESS CATALOGING-IN-PUBLICATION DATA

Web 2.0 / Lauri S. Friedman, book editor.
    p. cm. -- (Writing the critical essay: an opposing viewpoints guide)
Includes bibliographical references and index.
ISBN 978-0-7377-5026-3 (hardcover)
1. Web 2.0--Juvenile literature. 2. Online social networks--Juvenile literature. I. Friedman, Lauri S.
TK5105.88817.W418 2011
006.7'54--dc22
                                                                    2010033592

Printed in the United States of America
1 2 3 4 5 6 7 14 13 12 11 10

CONTENTS

Examining the state of writing and how it is taught in the United States was the official purpose of the National Commission on Writing in America's Schools and Colleges. The commission, made up of teachers, school administrators, business leaders, and college and university presidents, released its first report in 2003. "Despite the best efforts of many educators," commissioners argued, "writing has not received the full attention it deserves." Among the findings of the commission was that most fourth-grade students spent less than three hours a week writing, that three-quarters of high school seniors never receive a writing assignment in their history or social studies classes, and that more than 50 percent of first-year students in college have problems writing error-free papers. The commission called for a "cultural sea change" that would increase the emphasis on writing for both elementary and secondary schools. These conclusions have made some educators realize that writing must be emphasized in the curriculum. As colleges are demanding an ever-higher level of writing proficiency from incoming students, schools must respond by making students more competent writers. In response to these concerns, the SAT, an influential standardized test used for college admissions, required an essay for the first time in 2005.

Books in the Writing the Critical Essay: An Opposing Viewpoints Guide series use the patented Opposing Viewpoints format to help students learn to organize ideas and arguments and to write essays using common critical writing techniques. Each book in the series focuses on a particular type of essay writing—including expository, persuasive, descriptive, and narrative—that students learn while being taught both the five-paragraph essay as well as longer pieces of writing that have an opinionated focus. These guides include everything necessary to help students research, outline, draft, edit, and ultimately write successful essays across the curriculum, including essays for the SAT.

Using Opposing Viewpoints

This series is inspired by and builds upon Greenhaven Press's acclaimed Opposing Viewpoints series. As in the parent series, each book in the Writing the Critical Essay series focuses on a timely and controversial social issue that provides lots of opportunities for creating thought-provoking essays. The first section of each volume begins with a brief introductory essay that provides context for the opposing viewpoints that follow. These articles are chosen for their accessibility and clearly stated views. The thesis of each article is made explicit in the article's title and is accentuated by its pairing with an opposing or alternative view. These essays are both models of persuasive writing techniques and valuable research material that students can mine to write their own informed essays. Guided reading and discussion questions help lead students to key ideas and writing techniques presented in the selections.

The second section of each book begins with a preface discussing the format of the essays and examining characteristics of the featured essay type. Model five-paragraph and longer essays then demonstrate that essay type. The essays are annotated so that key writing elements and techniques are pointed out to the student. Sequential, step-by-step exercises help students construct and refine thesis statements; organize material into outlines; analyze and try out writing techniques; write transitions, introductions, and conclusions; and incorporate quotations and other researched material. Ultimately, students construct their own compositions using the designated essay type.

The third section of each volume provides additional research material and writing prompts to help the student. Additional facts about the topic of the book serve as a convenient source of supporting material for essays. Other features help students go beyond the book for their research. Like other Greenhaven Press books, each book in the Writing the Critical Essay series includes bibliographic listings of relevant periodical articles, books, Web sites, and organizations to contact.

Writing the Critical Essay: An Opposing Viewpoints Guide will help students master essay techniques that can be used in any discipline.

From Web 2.0 to Web 3.0

The first generation of the Internet was revolutionary, but it may not seem so by today's standards. The first sites displayed a static, reading-based approach to information, much like billboards or business cards. Home pages consisted of material that could not be changed or interacted with, and today's Internet user would likely find the first generation of content primitive, slow, and isolated. The next generation of the Internet, however—what has been dubbed Web 2.0—features sites and applications that make content interactive. This online era has been marked by the phenomenon of connecting users to one another via applications and sites such as Flickr, Digg, and Blogger, platforms that allow them to share and comment on a wide range of material. Indeed, Web 2.0 has demonstrated the power of and interest in social networks and has been characterized largely by collaboration: people collaborating to create and share information (as on Wikipedia), communities (as on Facebook), and content (as on YouTube).

While Web 2.0 has helped people connect with other *people*, the next generation of the Internet—which experts are tentatively calling Web 3.0—is expected to help people connect with *information*. Reporter Jonathan Richards explains the difference in the following way: "If Web 2.0 was all about harnessing the collective intelligence of crowds to give information a value—lots of people liked this story so you might too (Digg.com), people who like Madonna also like this artist (last.fm), lots of people linked to this site so that makes it the most relevant (Google's basic PageRank algorithm)—then Web 3.0 is about giving the Internet itself a brain."[1] Though there is much speculation about what exactly Web 3.0 will entail, most experts agree it will be highly intelligent, personalized, and portable.

Web 3.0 is sometimes described as "the Semantic Web," which refers to a version of the Internet in which words take on in-context meaning. Contrast this with current Internet searches, in which browsers are largely ignorant—users type specific keywords or phrases into a search engine, which spits out results without understanding their meaning or analyzing their content. A search for "Apple" yields pages on both computers and fruit; a search for "Saturn" returns pages on planets, mythology, and cars. If the word appears on a page, it is delivered to the user indiscriminately. "Right now, search engines can't tell the difference between Paris Hilton and the Hilton in Paris,"[2] says Jeff Bates, cofounder of Slashdot, a technology news site.

Web 3.0 browsers, however, will be able to search for information much more intelligently. For example, rather than visiting multiple sites and pages to select a movie, find showtimes, and then choose a nearby restaurant, Web 3.0 browsers are expected to understand and react to a complex phrase, such as, "I want to see an action movie and then eat at an upscale sushi restaurant. What choices do I have?" The browser of the future will analyze such a question, search the Internet for all possible data combinations (current releases, showtimes, restaurant locales, cuisines, driving routes), organize the possibilities, and deliver the results. "The idea is to move beyond mere keyword searches to a better understanding of natural-language queries,"[3] explains *PC* magazine writer Cade Metz.

The Web 3.0 browser is also expected to be highly personalized. With each search, the browser is expected to learn its user's preferences, tastes, likes, and dislikes—and will eventually make selections and recommendations based on these preferences. After a while, a user would not need to ask very specific questions to receive personalized results. One might simply type in "Where should I go for dinner?" After consulting a history of your past choices, it would suggest a list of restaurants tailored to your specific tastes. Web 3.0 browsers would be so personalized, in fact, that a search of the same question or phrase would result in completely different results sets on different users' computers. Says writer Jonathan Strickland, "Web 3.0 is going to be like having a personal assistant who knows practically everything about you and can access all the information on the Internet to answer any question."[4]

Finally, while Web 1.0 existed only on computers, and Web 2.0 has graduated to cell phones and handheld devices, Web 3.0 is expected to exist everywhere. Experts imagine a world in which household and personal devices—everything from ovens and microwaves to clothing and jewelry—are Internet based and ready to serve a user. Uplinked window shades are expected to know to open and close on the basis of the weather outside; smart jewelry is expected to be able to monitor a wearer's biopatterns to anticipate whether a heart attack or stroke is imminent. The portability of Web 3.0 is one of its main features, and once the technology exists to support it, the possibilities seem nearly limitless.

Yet with Web 3.0 is expected to come the barrage of controversies and problems that have been raised with each previous version of the Internet. As Web 2.0 has become pervasive and popular, for example, users have debated whether or not the new Internet irretrievably violates our privacy, threatens our children's neurological development, and hampers or enhances our personal relationships. The risk to journalism, art, and information has also been carefully questioned. These debates are likely to be expanded with Web 3.0 and whatever supersedes it. The model essays and viewpoints offered in *Writing the Critical Essay: Web 2.0* discuss the controversies surrounding social networking websites and content-sharing platforms that have characterized Web 2.0 and are also likely to define Web 3.0 and beyond. Thought-provoking essay questions and step-by-step writing exercises help readers write their own five-paragraph essays on this emerging topic.

Notes

1. Jonathan Richards, "Web 3.0 and Beyond: The Next 20 Years of the Internet," *London Times*, October 2007.
2. Quoted in Cade Metz, "Web 3.0: Semantics and Search," *PC*, March 14, 2007. www.pcmag.com/article2/0,2817,2102852,00.asp.
3. Metz, "Web 3.0." Semantics and Search.
4. Jonathan Strickland, "How Web 3.0 Will Work," HowStuffWorks.com, 2008. http://computer.howstuff works.com/web-302.htm.

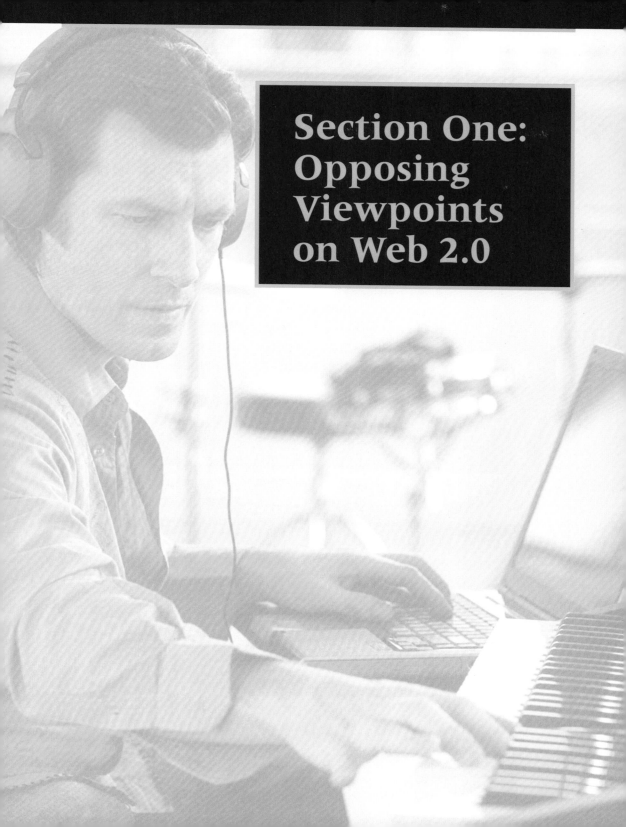

**Section One:
Opposing
Viewpoints
on Web 2.0**

Social Networking Improves Human Relationships

Jessica Misener

In the following viewpoint Jessica Misener argues that social networking improves human relationships. Although she acknowledges that some applications on sites such as Facebook are silly, indulgent wastes of time, Misener asserts that, in general, the use of such sites keeps people connected to each other and involved in each other's lives in meaningful ways and even helps them succeed professionally. Misener admits that social networking sites should not be the primary medium through which people have the bulk of their social interactions, yet she believes that social networking sites improve relationships that already exist and are integral to making the kinds of new connections that are critical for success in today's fast-paced world. She concludes that social networking sites are here to stay and argues that they positively affect both personal and professional relationships.

Jessica Misener writes about music, fashion, and social trends.

Consider the following questions:

1. How many people use the social networking site Facebook, according to Misener?
2. What did a 2007 Michigan State University study find about how Facebook affects its users, as cited by the author?
3. Who is Shelley E. Taylor and how does she factor into Misener's argument?

Jessica Misener, "In Defense of Facebook," *Relevant Magazine*, January 2010. Reproduced by permission.

I logged onto Facebook this morning and sinned.

Well, so I've been told by countless news articles, press releases and sermons. While our millennial generation has flocked to social networking, making it the hottest method of communication, others wax panic-stricken about how Facebook users (over 300 million of us) are devolving into socially awkward loners, whittling themselves into isolation against the glow of their laptop screens.

Although sites like Facebook have been criticized for supposedly creating a generation of loners, the author argues that social networking has its advantages as well.

Criticism of the Facebook Generation

Instead of chatting with someone over coffee, they say, we sit alone and blog about our problems. We Twitter our way through church, noses in our iPhones, then don't know what to say to anyone after the service. We find

Millions of People Use Social Networking Sites

The number of social networking site users has grown exponentially since the advent of the technology in 2002. As of 2009 Facebook had the most registered users of all the social networking sites.

Year	Members, Subscribers, Users	
2002	AOL	26,500,000
2003	Friendster	3,500,000
	AOL	24,300,000
2004	Facebook	1,000,000
	MySpace	1,000,000
	Friendster	7,000,000
	AOL	22,200,000
2005	Facebook	5,500,000
	Friendster	15,000,000
	AOL	19,500,000
	MySpace	45,000,000
2006	Twitter	100,000
	AOL	13,200,000
	Facebook	12,000,000
	Friendster	40,000,000
	MySpace	65,000,000
2007	Twitter	450,000
	AOL	9,300,000
	Facebook	50,000,000
	Friendster	75,000,000
	MySpace	100,000,000
2008	Twitter	1,000,000
	AOL	6,900,000
	Friendster	75,000,000
	MySpace	135,000,000
	Facebook	150,000,000
2009	AOL	5,100,000
	Twitter	30,000,000
	Friendster	110,000,000
	MySpace	150,000,000
	Facebook	300,000,000

Taken from: SEO Quotient.com, April 2010.

out about engagements and pregnancies first through Facebook. Our generation is too bloated with the milk of virtual interaction, so it goes, and we need solid social food before we degenerate into pixilated weirdos who can't carry on a face-to-face conversation.

As a blogger on the *Huffington Post* writes, "[Facebook] is overcrowded with attention-starved grown-ups essentially screaming. "Look at me . . . look at me!" all day long. They change their profile photos as often as I change my underwear, and they've somehow convinced themselves that their lives are infinitely interesting all the time."

Ouch. I'd be offended, but my last status update explored the titillating subject of my Converse sneakers. Maybe the naysayers have a point. After all, Twittering to your husband will never be the same as giving him a hug. A stream of status updates does not a flesh-and-blood friendship make.

> ## Social Networking Breaks Down Isolation
>
> While the majority of teens use sites such as MySpace and Facebook to hang out with people they already know in real life, a smaller portion uses them to find like-minded people. Before social networking, the one kid in school who was, say, a fan of Godzilla or progressive politics might find himself isolated. These days, that youngster has peers everywhere.
>
> Karen Goldberg Goff, "Social Networking Benefits Validated," *Washington Times*, January 28, 2009.

Millions of Users Cannot Be Wrong

But Facebook, like it or not, is here to stay. The number of people who use social networking sites has doubled since 2007, and Twitter recently hit more than 7 billion cumulative tweets. A stumble through the graveyard of sites that have already come and gone (Friendster, Myspace) indicates that social networking is the main powerhouse in our culture's new way of virtual life, so we'd do well to examine the upside. Is it really possible that Farmville can cultivate our souls? Can writing "happy birthday" on my friends' walls be a spiritual discipline?

Perhaps. Social networking has some marked advantages:

1. *It really does help you keep in touch.* A 2007 study at Michigan State University found that Facebook boosted

"social capital" for members with low self-esteem and low levels of life-satisfaction. Most of us have been pleasantly surprised to reconnect with a long lost friend from second grade or catch up with a long-distance cousin. Through Facebook, I've received party invitations, heard about high school reunion plans and found out that scores of my friends of yesteryear have relocated to New York, making it easy for us to meet up. In these frantically busy and digitally pulsing times, sometimes social networking can help us put the brakes on the rat race and take a few moments to make time for those around us.

The New Face of Business

2. *It's good for business.* Any business worth its 21st-century cred these days has to have a Facebook page and a Twitter account, and several corporations are hiring full-time "social media directors" to manage their accounts. Yep, your re-tweeting skills could potentially land you a plush gig! As a writer, I use Facebook to link to articles I've written, which generates way more hits than if I abandoned it to the hope of idle Web surfers stumbling upon my portfolio. I even boldly Facebooked a *New York Times* writer I admire, and to my surprise he replied (he didn't respond to my over-eager follow-up message to which I attached samples of my work, but I like to think he was too busy harvesting virtual raspberries).

For those who often work alone, like freelancers or graduate students, social networking can be a valuable way to make connections and maintain a professional community. As career-minded young adults, who wants to miss out on that?

Social Networking Helps People Feel Less Alone

3. *It makes you feel less alone.* I know you've been there: it's 11 P.M., you're at your desk, bored and lonely. You keep

Social networking can ease the transition to new places until new friends are made.

constantly refreshing Facebook so that you see everyone's status updates as they were posted 6 seconds ago. Suddenly, someone IMs you or comments on your page, and you're feeling better. Does that make you attention-starved, or does it just mean you're experiencing a unique facet of friendship?

"Creating [social] networks to ease the transition to new places can be hugely helpful to people, offsetting loneliness until new friends are made," psychology professor Shelley E. Taylor tells *Newsweek*. The Facebook arena can be just as valid a place to practice agape [AH-guh-pay: selfless love] and "turning the other cheek" as your office or your home. When you next log on, commit to reaching out to five people's pages or profiles before you post news of your own.

Obviously, there's the lurking danger of overdosing on social networking. Facebook is a useful tool, not a lifestyle choice, and it should never snowball into your only method of communicating with others. But if you're keeping a well-balanced emotional and spiritual life, don't fret that Tweeting is sending you into a misanthropic tornado of geekdom. Sometimes all things—even virtual things—can be used for good.

Analyze the essay:

1. The author recounts how she successfully Facebooked a *New York Times* writer she admires. Have you ever reached out to a stranger you admire on a social networking site? If so, what was the situation? Was the person famous? Did you get a response? How did the interaction make you feel? Using this personal experience as evidence, write one to two paragraphs on whether you think social networking sites are useful for facilitating new and important relationships.

2. Misener argues that people use social networking sites to feel less lonely, stay in touch with each other, and further their careers. How do you think Elizabeth Bernstein, author of the following essay, would specifically counter each of these claims? Which author provided better evidence for their argument? After reading both essays, state with which author you ultimately agree.

Social Networking Threatens Human Relationships

Elizabeth Bernstein

Social networking sites dumb down personal communications and threaten real-life relationships, argues Elizabeth Bernstein in the following viewpoint. She complains that only rarely do sites like Facebook meaningfully connect people; more often, they are used as a platform for people to share boring and inane information about their day-to-day lives. She resents that many people waste hours on social networking sites yet claim to be too busy to pick up the phone to call their friends or family, or even to write them a substantial e-mail. In Bernstein's opinion, it is wrong to forgo meaningful communication for the sake of forwarding quizzes, videos, or random comments about one's day. For all these reasons, Bernstein concludes that social networking sites offer little that is positive or meaningful for personal relationships.

Elizabeth Bernstein is a staff writer for the *Wall Street Journal*.

Consider the following questions:

1. What example does Bernstein give of how Facebook users share information that is too personal, or even disgusting?
2. Who is Gwen Jewett and how do her comments help support the author's argument?
3. What types of conduct changes does Bernstein say might improve the significance of social networking interactions?

Notice to my friends: I love you all dearly.

But I don't give a hoot that you are "having a busy Monday," your child "took 30 minutes to brush his teeth," your dog "just ate an ant trap" or you want to "save the piglets." And I really, really don't care which Addams Family member you most resemble. (I could have told you the answer before you took the quiz on Facebook.)

Here's where you and I went wrong: We took our friendship online. First we began communicating more by email than by phone. Then we switched to "instant messaging" or "texting." We "friended" each other on Facebook, and began communicating by "tweeting" our thoughts—in 140 characters or less—via Twitter.

A Threat to Real-Life Relationships

All this online social networking was supposed to make us closer. And in some ways it has. Thanks to the Internet, many of us have gotten back in touch with friends from high school and college, shared old and new photos, and become better acquainted with some people we might never have grown close to offline.

Last year, when a friend of mine was hit by a car and went into a coma, his friends and family were able to easily and instantly share news of his medical progress—and send well wishes and support—thanks to a Web page his mom created for him.

But there's a danger here, too. If we're not careful, our online interactions can hurt our real-life relationships.

Like many people, I'm experiencing Facebook Fatigue. I'm tired of loved ones—you know who you are—who claim they are too busy to pick up the phone, or even write a decent email, yet spend hours on social-media sites, uploading photos of their children or parties, forwarding inane quizzes, posting quirky, sometimes nonsensical one-liners or tweeting their latest whereabouts. ("Anyone know a good restaurant in Berlin?")

One of the big problems is how we converse. Typing still leaves something to be desired as a communication tool; it lacks the nuances that can be expressed by body language and voice inflection. "Online, people can't see the yawn," says Patricia Wallace, a psychologist at Johns Hopkins University's Center for Talented Youth and author of *The Psychology of the Internet*.

Some people will spend hours on social media sites but claim that they are too busy to spend time with or even call their friends and family.

Social Networking Makes Us Boring

But let's face it, the problem is much greater than which tools we use to communicate. It's what we are actually saying that's really mucking up our relationships. "Oh my God, a college friend just updated her Facebook status to say that her 'teeth are itching for a flossing!'" shrieked a friend of mine recently. "That's gross. I don't want to hear about what's going on inside her mouth."

That prompted me to check my own Facebook page, only to find that three of my pals—none of whom know each other—had the exact same status update: "Zzzzzzz." They promptly put me to "zzzzzzz."

This brings us to our first dilemma: Amidst all this heightened chatter, we're not saying much that's interesting, folks. Rather, we're breaking a cardinal rule of companionship: Thou Shalt Not Bore Thy Friends.

"It's called narcissism," says Matt Brown, a 36-year-old business-development manager for a chain of hair salons and spas in Seattle. He's particularly annoyed by a friend who works at an auto dealership who tweets every time he sells a car, a married couple who bicker on Facebook's public walls and another couple so "mooshy-gooshy" they sit in the same room of their house posting love messages to each other for all to see. "Why is your life so frickin' important and entertaining that we need to know?" Mr. Brown says.

Gwen Jewett, for her part, is sick of meal status updates. "A few of my friends like to post several times a day about what they are eating: 'I just ate a Frito pie.' 'I am enjoying a double hot-fudge sundae at home tonight.' 'Just ate a whole pizza with sausage, peppers and double cheese,'" says the 49-year-old career coach in suburban Dallas. "My question is this: If we didn't call each other on the phone every time we ate before, why do we need the alerts now?"

Too Much Information

For others, boredom isn't the biggest challenge of managing Internet relationships. Consider, for example, how people you know often seem different online—not just gussied up or more polished, but bolder, too, displaying sides of their personalities you have never seen before.

Antisocial Networking?

Having been relegated to our screens, are our friendships now anything more than a form of distraction? When they've shrunk to the size of a wall post, do they retain any content? If we have 768 "friends," in what sense do we have any?

William Deresiewicz, "Faux Friendship," *Chronicle of Higher Education*, December 6, 2009.

Alex Gilbert, 27, who works for a nonprofit in Houston that teaches creative writing to kids, is still puzzling over an old friend—"a particularly masculine-type dude"—who plays in a heavy-metal band and heads a motorcycle club yet posts videos on Facebook of "uber cute" kittens. "It's not fodder for your real-life conversation," Mr. Gilbert says. "We're not going to get together and talk about how cute kittens are."

Social Networking Has Not Significantly Improved Americans' Lives

Out of all the technological advances over the past decade, Americans think social networking sites and blogs have not made as much positive difference in their lives as have cell phones, e-mail, or the Internet.

Question: "Has the following technology been a change for the better, a change for the worse, or not made much difference?"

Type of Technology	Change for the better %	Change for the worse %	Not much difference %	Unsure %
Cell phones	69%	14%	11%	5%
E-mail	65%	7%	19%	9%
The Internet	65%	16%	11%	8%
Handheld devices such as BlackBerries and iPhones	56%	25%	12%	7%
Online shopping	54%	15%	24%	8%
Social networking sites such as Facebook	35%	21%	31%	12%
Internet blogs	29%	21%	36%	14%

Taken from: Pew Research Center Poll, December 9–13, 2009.

James Hills discovered that a colleague is gay via Facebook, but he says that didn't bother him. It was after his friend joined groups that cater to hairy men, such as "Furball NYC," that he was left feeling awkward. "This is something I just didn't need to know," says Mr. Hills, who is 32 and president of a marketing firm in Elgin, Ill. "I'd feel the same way if it was a straight friend joining a leather-and-lace group."

And then there's jealousy. In all that information you're posting about your life—your vacation, your kids, your promotions at work, even that margarita you just drank—someone is bound to find something to envy. When it comes to relationships, such online revelations can make breaking up even harder to do.

"Facebook prolongs the period it takes to get over someone, because you have an open window into their life, whether you want to or not," says Yianni Garcia of New York, a consultant who helps companies use social media. "You see their updates, their pictures and their relationship status."

Encouraging Mean-Spirited Behavior

Mr. Garcia, 24, felt the sting of Facebook jealousy personally last spring, after he split up with his boyfriend. For a few weeks, he continued to visit his ex's Facebook page, scrutinizing his new friends. Then one day he discovered that his former boyfriend had blocked him from accessing his profile.

Why? "He said he'd only 'unfriended' me to protect himself, because if someone flirted with me he would feel jealous," Mr. Garcia says.

Facebook can also be a mecca for passive-aggressive behavior. "Suddenly, things you wouldn't say out loud in conversation are OK to say because you're sitting behind a computer screen," says Kimberly Kaye, 26, an arts writer in New York. She was surprised when friends who had politely discussed health-care reform over dinner later grew much more antagonistic when they continued the argument online.

Just ask Heather White. She says her college roommate at the University of Georgia started an argument over text about who should clean their apartment. Ms. White, 22, who was home visiting her parents at the time, asked her friend to call her so they could discuss the issue. Her friend never did.

A few days later, Ms. White, who graduated in May, updated her Facebook status, commenting that her favorite country duo, Brooks & Dunn, just broke up. Almost immediately, her roommate responded, writing publicly on her wall: "Just like us." The two women have barely spoken since then.

A Need to Change Conduct

So what's the solution, short of "unfriending" or "unfollowing" everyone who annoys you? You can use the "hide" button on Facebook to stop getting your friends' status updates—they'll never know—or use TwitterSnooze, a website that allows you to temporarily suspend tweets from someone you follow. (Warning: They'll get a notice from Twitter when you begin reading their tweets again.)

The Facebook live feed status allows people to constantly update friends with the events of everyday life, most of which are self-involved and arbitrary, in the author's opinion.

But these are really just Band-Aid tactics. To improve our interactions, we need to change our conduct, not just cover it up. First, watch your own behavior, asking yourself before you post anything: "Is this something I'd want someone to tell me?" "Run it by that focus group of one," says Johns Hopkins's Dr. Wallace.

And positively reward others, responding only when they write something interesting, ignoring them when they are boring or obnoxious. (Commenting negatively will only start a very public war.)

If all that fails, you can always start a new group: "Get Facebook to Create an Eye-Roll Button Now!"

Analyze the essay:

1. Bernstein argues that people use social networking sites for silly, self-indulgent purposes. Think about the way you and your friends use such sites. What percentage of this use would you say is for important endeavors, such as professional, political, social, artistic, or significantly personal things? What percentage would you say is for self-aggrandizing, narcissistic, gossipy, or mean-spirited endeavors? Use what you come up with to write one paragraph on whether you think social networking sites are used largely for important or unimportant purposes.

2. Bernstein quotes from several sources to support the points she makes in her essay. Make a list of all the people she quotes, including their credentials and the nature of their comments. Then pick the quote you found most persuasive. Why did you choose it? What did it lend to Bernstein's argument?

Web 2.0 Applications Threaten Journalism

Neil Henry

In the following viewpoint Neil Henry argues that Web 2.0 applications such as blogs and video-sharing sites threaten the quality of journalism. He discusses how newspapers have been forced to lay off hundreds of skilled journalists because the Internet has stolen valuable sources of revenue. As a result, society has significantly fewer trained professionals to break important news stories, expose scandals, and report the news in a fair and independent manner. Henry explains that a skilled journalistic force is integral to a democratic society—in fact, journalism is so important to society it should be regarded as a public good. In his opinion, untrained bloggers and "citizen journalists"—ordinary individuals with access to a camera and the Internet—are no substitute for trained professionals, because such people have neither the resources nor skills to deliver fair, unbiased, and deeply researched stories. Henry warns that if America does not protect the craft of journalism, everyone in society will suffer.

Neil Henry is a professor of journalism at the University of California, Berkeley. He is the author of *American Carnival: Journalism Under Siege in an Age of New Media*.

Consider the following questions:

1. In what main way has the advent of the Internet threatened the survival of newspapers, according to Henry?
2. What kinds of news stories does the author say bloggers and citizen journalists are unable to report on? Name at least two of the examples he gives.
3. Who does Henry say are like modern-day pirates?

Neil Henry, "The Decline of News," *San Francisco Chronicle*, May 29, 2007, p. B-5.
Copyright © 2007 Hearst Communications Inc. Reproduced by permission of the author.

The *[San Francisco] Chronicle*'s announcement earlier this month [May 2007] that 100 newsroom jobs will be slashed in the coming weeks in the face of mounting financial woes represents just the latest chapter in a tragic story of traditional journalism's decline.

Reportedly losing an estimated $1 million a week, the paper's owner, the Hearst Corp., concluded it had no recourse but to trim costs by laying off reporters, editors and other skilled professionals, or offering buyouts to the most seasoned journalists in order to induce them to leave. The cuts reportedly will amount to a quarter of the *Chronicle*'s editorial staff.

In the age of "new" media, this rollback in "old" media may be among the most drastic in recent memory, but it is nothing new to the public.

The Internet Has Undermined Newspapers

Indeed, across the country newspapers have suffered enormous financial losses over the past decade, with far fewer professionals today covering the news locally, nationally and internationally as a result of the industry's contraction.

The factors behind this shrinkage are sadly familiar: The rise of the Internet has produced sharp declines in traditional advertising revenues in the printed press. Free online advertising competitors such as Craigslist .com have sharply undermined classified advertising as a traditional source of revenue. While many newspapers have attempted mightily to forge a presence on the Web—including the *Chronicle*, whose terrific sfgate .com is among the top 10 most trafficked news sites in America—revenue from online advertising is paltry compared to that from traditional print sources. As a result, newspapers such as the *Chronicle* must make staff cuts to survive—and increasingly it is highly skilled professional journalists committed to seeking the truth and reporting it, independently and without fear or favor, who must go.

Fewer Journalists Means Less Quality News

The average citizen may not realize how severely the public's access to important news, gathered according to high standards, may be threatened by these bottom line trade-offs.

When journalists' jobs are eliminated, especially as many as the *Chronicle* intends, the product is inevitably less than it was. The fact is there will be nothing on YouTube, or in the blogosphere, or anywhere else on the Web to effectively replace the valuable work of those professionals.

Fewer resources will be available to investigate stories as nationally significant as the BALCO scandal,[1] for example; fewer professionals to doggedly uncover shady

Craigslist.com and other free online advertising competitors have undercut classified advertising, which previously was a large source of revenue for newspapers.

---

1. The Bay Area Laboratory Cooperative scandal, in which professional athletes were found to be using steroids.

financial practices at the University of California, forcing top officials to publicly acknowledge their mistakes and work to fix them; fewer journalists to cover local city halls, courts and schools, reporting community news that the public often takes for granted—and which other media, including local television and radio outlets, rely upon to set their own news priorities.

There certainly won't be any less news or fewer scandals to report, mind you: Only fewer trained watchdogs on hand to do the hard work of hunting, finding and reporting it.

Real Journalism Is an Endangered Skill

Idolaters of Web-based news and information sites, "citizen"-produced journalism, and the blogosphere of individual self-publishers, often argue that old mainstays such as the *Chronicle* are, in fact, getting only what they deserve.

If "old" media cannot successfully adjust to the digital age, too bad, these critics argue. The corporate media were never that good in the first place, they say, and have failed us miserably in the past. There are plenty of alternatives on the Web to take traditional journalism's place, including the millions of bloggers opining about the news, not to mention powerful news aggregators such as Google and Yahoo whose computerized search robots harvest riches of news and other content provided by others—and generate billions of dollars in annual profits for their owners.

As a teacher of journalism, I see the situation differently. I see a world where the craft of reporting the news fairly and independently is very much endangered; and with it a society increasingly fractured,

---

Amateur Journalists Will Get the Brush-Off, Not the News

I am offended to think that anyone, anywhere believes that American institutions as insulated, self-preserving, and self-justifying as police departments, school systems, legislatures, and chief executives can be held to [account] . . . by amateurs, pursuing the task without compensation, training, or for that matter, sufficient standing to make public officials even care to whom it is they are lying or from whom they are withholding information.

David Simon, quoted in Chris Hogg, "Did the Internet Kill Journalism?" *Digital Journal*, May 11, 2009.

Newspaper Closures in the United States

Since 2007 more than 180 newspapers have closed or stopped publishing a print edition, resulting in the loss of more than 34,000 jobs. Newspapers that have closed or stopped publishing a newsprint edition include:

Albuquerque Tribune	*L.A. City Beat*
Ann Arbor News	*New York Blade*
Asian Week	*New York Sun*
Baltimore Examiner	*Rocky Mountain News*
Christian Science Monitor	*Seattle Post-Intelligencer*
Cincinnati Post	*Tucson Citizen*
Kentucky Post	*USA Today International Edition*
Detroit Daily Press	*Washington Blade*

Taken from: Paper Cuts, April 20, 2010. http://newspaperlayoffs.com.

less informed by fact and more susceptible to political and marketing propaganda, cant and bias.

Profit Should Not Drive Journalism

I see a world in which the pursuit of truth in service of the public interest is declining as a cultural value in our society amid this technological tumult; a world where professional journalism, practiced according to widely accepted ethical values, is a rapidly diminishing feature in our expanding news and information systems, as we escape to the Web to experience the latest "new" thing.

I see a world where corporations such as Google and Yahoo continue to enrich themselves with little returning to journalistic enterprises, all this ultimately at the expense of legions of professional reporters across

The author argues that search engines like Google and Yahoo! are contributing to the decline of traditional journalism.

America, now out of work because their employers in "old" media could not afford to pay them.

Not long ago, billionaire real estate executive Sam Zell, who earlier this year [2007] purchased the Tribune Co. family of newspapers, including the *Los Angeles Times*, made this point quite bluntly. He likened Google and Yahoo to modern-day pirates ripping off treasure produced by others. According to the *Washington Post*, Zell told a gathering at Stanford University in April, "If all the newspapers in America did not allow Google to steal their content, how profitable would Google be? Not very."

For their part, Google executives maintain that the travails of the American newspaper industry today are hardly their fault. They argue that their informational enterprises simply help the public find whatever it is looking for. They insist that the problems of newspapers are the result of market forces, driven by the continuing technological revolution.

Indeed last week [mid-May 2007], at a conference on the state of American newspapers at Stanford, Google Vice President Marissa Mayer reportedly made this argument quite clearly. She said simply: "We are computer scientists, not journalists."

While that may be true, the time has come for corporations such as Google to accept more responsibility for the future of American journalism, in recognition of the threat "computer science" poses to journalism's place in a democratic society.

Society Needs Real Journalists

It is no longer acceptable for Google corporate executives to say that they don't practice journalism, they only work to provide links to "content providers." Journalism is not just a matter of jobs, and dollars and cents lost. It is a public trust vital to a free society. It stands to reason that Google and corporations like it, who indirectly benefit so enormously from the expensive labor of journalists, should begin to take on greater civic responsibility for journalism's plight. Is it possible for Google to somehow engage and support the traditional news industry and important local newspapers more fully, for example, to become a vital part of possible solutions to this crisis instead of a part of the problem?

Is it not possible for Google and other information corporations to offer more direct support to schools of journalism to help ensure that this craft's values and skills are passed on to the next generation?

Is it not possible for these flourishing corporations to assist and identify more closely with the work of venerable organizations, such as the Society of Professional Journalists, in support of their mission and to preserve this important calling? I like to think such things are possible.

Meantime, I can't help but fear a future, increasingly barren of skilled journalists, in which Google "news" searches turn up not news, but the latest snarky rants from basement bloggers, fake news reports from government officials and PR cleverly peddled in the guise of journalism by advertisers wishing only to sell, sell, sell.

Analyze the essay:

1. The author of this essay is a former reporter for the *Washington Post*. He is also a professor of journalism at one of America's top communciations schools. In what way does knowing his professional background influence your opinion of his argument? Does it make you more or less likely to agree with his opinion on this topic? Why?

2. Henry argues that Google and other Internet information companies have an obligation to support the traditional news industry. In a few sentences, flesh out what he means by this. Then, state whether or not you agree.

Web 2.0 Applications Improve Journalism

Bernard Lunn

In the following viewpoint Bernard Lunn argues that the Internet is changing, but not killing, journalism. He admits that Web 2.0 applications have threatened traditional models of journalism such as newspapers and have cost reporters their jobs. But Lunn says there is no reason why bloggers and citizen journalists cannot deliver quality news. The traits that make up journalism—the desire to get to the bottom of a story, expose the truth, learn more about a situation, and do so with honor and integrity—need not exist solely in professionally trained people, according to Lunn. In fact, he contends that the Internet has created the opportunity for countless Americans to embrace these traits and report on the day's events. Lunn says it is reasonable to expect a technology as amazing as the Internet to change the way news is reported. He argues that a new model of journalism is emerging that will both continue America's tradition of great journalism and offer opportunities for employment.

Bernard Lunn is the chief operating officer of ReadWriteWeb, a blog that provides news, reviews, and analysis of Web technology trends.

Consider the following questions:

1. In what way are print or television news sources like bathwater, according to Lunn?
2. What four traits does the author say have inspired countless journalists, both trained and untrained?
3. Why does Lunn see no need to protect journalism with public money or grants?

Bernard Lunn, "Journalism 2.0: Don't Throw Out the Baby," ReadWriteWeb.com, April 30, 2009. Reproduced by permission.

When I was a kid, I wanted to be a journalist. My heroes were people like Woodward and Bernstein[1] and the people reporting from war zones. The profession seemed to be both glamorous and worthwhile. Faced with a real decision as a young adult, I went into the IT [information technology] industry. Then, later in my career, I started blogging, and then writing for ReadWriteWeb, and now I am COO [chief operating officer] of this news media business. So that got me thinking about the past, present, and future of journalism. . . .

A New Journalistic Model Is Emerging

Blogging is open to anyone. You do not need to be trained as a journalist, nor do you need a job that pays you to blog. But many bloggers have created media businesses that employ people, cover the news on a regular basis, and sell advertising. They have created newspapers without the paper. Which turns out to be a fairly good business, with overheads low enough to make a reasonable profit.

However, the imperatives that come with running a real business tend to shift bloggers from the classic blog mode to something else. This has generated a lot of anguish among blog veterans who worry that blogging is "losing its soul." Journalists, on the other hand, face a starker, more existential threat as newspapers close shop.

So neither bloggers nor journalists are happy today.

But my optimistic nature inclines me to the view that some new model will emerge that makes for a fulfilling and reasonably well-compensated career.

Blogging Compared to Journalism

Blogging seems wonderful compared to traditional journalism: anybody can do it; the style is informal, fun, and personal; no editor has control of your voice; you're not

---

1. Bob Woodward and Carl Bernstein, the *Washington Post* reporters who broke the Watergate scandal in the early 1970s, which led to President Richard Nixon's resignation.

tied to a fixed schedule; and you encounter incredible diversity.

But now that many bloggers have morphed into small-media business owners, they are starting to feel pressure to follow a schedule and cover key news stories. This is a world that a traditionally trained journalist can recognize.

But there is a fundamental difference. Bloggers are passionate experts first and journalists second. Somebody who blogs about technology could not credibly switch to politics, and vice versa. The journalism profession is adept at taking somebody from a story on a bank robbery and allocating them to a political sex scandal. Their professional skills enable journalists to be switch-hitters.

This difference is generally advantageous to bloggers. Training somebody in the basics of journalism is easier than creating passionate expertise in a subject.

However, this is where the blog media business is in danger of throwing out the baby with the bathwater.

The investigative and opinionated pieces featured on some blogs are increasingly competing with those found in newspapers.

Journalistic Curiosity Can Exist in Anyone

We don't need print or TV to deliver news. Throw out the bathwater.

But the baby is cute. Let's keep the baby. Let's keep all the good things about journalism, the things that inspired me as a kid and that have inspired countless journalists:

1. A really strong desire to find the truth, wherever it may lurk;
2. An assumption that everyone knows more than you, and that your job is to find, cultivate, question, and listen to your sources, and then come to a view;
3. An inclination not to take anything at face value, because everyone has a point of view, and those points of view are usually driven by self-interest;
4. A resolve not to let commercial interests (in other words, advertisers) influence your search for the truth. . . .

"Journalism Is Still Just a Job"

I have always been in the technology business. I like writing about the technology business because I find it fascinating and there are a lot of really smart people to talk to. But techies can spout the most self-interested baloney when it comes to content. The Web 2.0 vision of user-generated content is millions of passionate experts creating content that really clever algorithms deliver to audiences. The people who create those really clever algorithms become rich beyond the dreams of avarice while throwing a few crumbs to the content creators. Don't try paying a mortgage with [Internet advertising model] AdSense or other CPC [cost per click]-affiliate revenue deals.

Citizen Journalists Get the News Big Media Ignores

Some community Web sites are beating local newspapers and TV to big stories. And citizen journalists of all stripes are looking deeply into niche topics that big media ignore or cover shallowly.

Dan Gillmor, "Journalism Isn't Dying, It's Reviving," *San Francisco Chronicle*, June 7, 2007.

To a techie, "content" is just something to throw in a software system. Content creators don't talk about "content." They talk about their art or craft. Journalism is a form of art, albeit closer to craft than art. To a techie, art is just content. Which is more important, code or art? If you had to choose between a world without computers or a world without art, which would you choose?

But let's not get carried away with this. Journalism is still just a job.

Journalism Is Not Dead, Just Changing

Would citizen journalists have exposed Watergate?

Yes, they would have.

We don't need to protect journalism with public money or grants. The greater social good will be delivered by thousands of people on the ground reporting what is happening. That massive flow will be analyzed and edited ("curated") by a small number of experts who are motivated and trained to uncover the truth.

Blogging, as opposed to traditional journalism, allows for more informal and personal writing without an editor to control the writer's voice.

What Online News Sources Do People Use?

On a typical day, the average consumer of online news uses two, three or as many as six of the following types of sources.

	All online news users 18+
A portrait website like GoogleNews, AOL, or Topix that gathers news from many different sources	56%
A website of a TV news organization such as CNN, Fox, or CBS	46%
A website that specializes in a particular topic like health, politics, or entertainment	38%
A website of a national or local newspaper	38%
An individual or organization, other than a journalist or news organization, that you follow on a social networking site like Facebook	30%
A website of an international news organization such as the BBC or the *Guardian,* or a foreign language news site	18%
A website that offers a mix of news and commentary, such as the Drudge Report or the Huffington Post	17%
The website of a radio news organization such as NPR	15%
A news podcast from an organization such as NPR or the *New York Times*	14%
A news organization or an individual journalist you follow on a social networking site like Facebook	13%
The website of an individual blogger (who does not work for a major news organization)	11%
A news website such as Digg or NewsTrust where users rank stories	7%
Twitter updates from an individual or organization other than a journalist or news organization	6%
Twitter updates from a journalist or news organization	4%
Use none of these on a typical day	14%
Use one to two of these on a typical day	34%
Use three to five of these on a typical day	36%
Use six or more on a typical day	16%

Taken from: Internet & American Life Project and Project for Excellence in Journalism Online, News Survey, December 28, 2006–January 18, 2010.

It won't be perfect. But the current system isn't perfect either. It is fair to say, though, that scumbags won't rest any easier. They will still be exposed.

Sacrifices will be made. One cannot imagine foreign bureaus surviving in anything close to their current form. Instead of having a few stringers on a loose contract, media firms will have a standardized deal that applies to anyone who covers fast-breaking news. That way, whoever is on the spot becomes a "just-in-time stringer."

Is that better or worse than what we have now? It's worse for the people working today in foreign bureaus on good salaries. But mostly, it's just different.

Analyze the essay:

1. In this essay, Lunn says journalism is important, but he argues it is still "just a job." What do you think Neil Henry, author of the previous essay, would have to say about this characterization? After reading both essays, with which author do you agree about journalism's status? Why?

2. Lunn and Henry disagree on whether journalism should benefit from support from outside parties such as the government or Internet corporations. Sum up each writer's position. Then, state with which author you agree. What piece of evidence did you find most persuasive? Why?

3. In making his argument, Lunn asks his readers, "If you had to choose between a world without computers or a world without art, which would you choose?" In one to two paragraphs, answer his question. What is more important to you: technology or art? Or, is the choice a false one? Explain your reasoning.

Web 2.0 Applications Erode the Quality of Information and Art

Andrew Keen

In the following viewpoint Andrew Keen warns that the Internet threatens the quality of information and art. Keen discusses how Web 2.0 applications have given everyone with a computer the means to write, make music, shoot video, and otherwise express themselves. But in Keen's opinion, this is not necessarily good for art or information. In the past, only the most talented individuals had their works published. But because Web 2.0 applications allow anyone to create and inform, the world is saturated with low-quality productions. For this reason, Keen worries that true art will get lost among the low-quality creations of the masses and that American society will fail to produce high-quality products, films, books, poetry, and art as it has in the past.

Andrew Keen is an entrepreneur and digital media critic. He hosts a podcast chat show at aftertv.com in which he discusses media, culture, and technology.

Consider the following questions:

1. In what way does Keen say Web 2.0 technology encourages even the most poorly educated and inarticulate Americans to express themselves?
2. In what way did dystopian authors Aldous Huxley, Ray Bradbury, and George Orwell get the future wrong, according to the author?
3. Why specifically does Keen think it is problematic for everyone to be an author?

L ast week, I was treated to lunch at a fashionable Japanese restaurant in Palo Alto by a serial Silicon Valley entrepreneur who, back in the dot.com boom, had invested in my start-up Audiocafe.com. The entrepreneur, like me a Silicon Valley veteran, was pitching me his latest start-up: a technology platform that creates easy-to-use software tools for online communities to publish weblogs, digital movies, and music. It is technology that enables anyone with a computer to become an author, a film director, or a musician. This Web 2.0 dream is Socrates's nightmare: technology that arms every citizen with the means to be an opinionated artist or writer.

"This is historic," my friend promised me. "We are enabling Internet users to author their own content. Think of it as empowering citizen media. We can help smash the elitism of the Hollywood studios and the big record labels. Our technology platform will radically democratize culture, build authentic community, create citizen media." Welcome to Web 2.0. . . .

Enabling Everyone to Create Is Not Necessarily Good

So what, exactly, is the Web 2.0 movement? As an ideology, it is based upon a series of ethical assumptions about media, culture, and technology. It worships the creative amateur: the self-taught filmmaker, the dorm-room musician, the unpublished writer. It suggests that everyone—even the most poorly educated and inarticulate amongst us—can and should use digital media to express and realize themselves. Web 2.0 "empowers" our creativity, it "democratizes" media, it "levels the playing field" between experts and amateurs. The enemy of Web 2.0 is "elitist" traditional media.

Empowered by Web 2.0 technology, we can all become citizen journalists, citizen videographers, citizen musicians. Empowered by this technology, we will be able to write in the morning, direct movies in the afternoon, and make music in the evening. . . .

The ideology of the Web 2.0 movement was perfectly summarized at the Technology Education and Design (TED) show in Monterey, [California,] last year [2005], when Kevin Kelly, Silicon Valley's über-idealist and author of the Web 1.0 Internet utopia *New Rules for The New Economy*, said:

> Imagine Mozart before the technology of the piano. Imagine Van Gogh before the technology of affordable oil paints. Imagine Hitchcock before the technology of film. We have a moral obligation to develop technology.

But where Kelly sees a moral obligation to develop technology, we should actually have—if we really care about Mozart, Van Gogh and Hitchcock—a moral obligation to question the development of technology.

We Do Not Need More of Ourselves

The consequences of Web 2.0 are inherently dangerous for the vitality of culture and the arts. Its empowering promises play upon that legacy of the '60s—the creeping narcissism that [historian] Christopher Lasch described so presciently, with its obsessive focus on the realization of the self.

Another word for narcissism is "personalization." Web 2.0 technology personalizes culture so that it reflects ourselves rather than the world around us. Blogs personalize media content so that all we read are our own thoughts. Online stores personalize our preferences, thus feeding back to us our own taste. Google personalizes searches so that all we see are advertisements for products and services we already use.

Instead of Mozart, Van Gogh, or Hitchcock, all we get with the Web 2.0 revolution is more of ourselves. . . .

The Problem with Democratizing Talent

The consequences of the digital media revolution are . . . profound. Apple and Google and Craigslist really are revolutionizing our cultural habits, our ways of entertaining ourselves, our ways of defining who we are. Traditional "elitist" media is being destroyed by digital technologies. Newspapers are in freefall. Network television, the modern equivalent of the dinosaur, is being shaken by TiVo's overnight annihilation of the 30-second commercial. The iPod is undermining the multibillion dollar music industry. Meanwhile, digital piracy, enabled by Silicon Valley hardware and justified by Silicon Valley intellectual property communists such as [law professor] Larry Lessig, is draining revenue from established artists, movie studios, newspapers, record labels, and song writers.

Is this a bad thing? The purpose of our media and culture industries—beyond the obvious need to make

YouTube, a Web 2.0 application, permits anyone with a computer to shoot short movies, shows, and other types of video.

money and entertain people—is to discover, nurture, and reward elite talent. Our traditional mainstream media has done this with great success over the last century. Consider Alfred Hitchcock's masterpiece, *Vertigo* and a couple of other brilliantly talented works of the same name: the 1999 book called *Vertigo*, by Anglo-German writer W.G. Sebald, and the 2004 song "Vertigo," by Irish rock star Bono. Hitchcock could never have made his expensive, complex movies outside the Hollywood studio system. Bono would never have become Bono without the music industry's super-heavyweight marketing muscle. And W.G. Sebald, the most obscure of this trinity of talent, would have remained an unknown university professor had a high-end publishing house not had the good taste to discover and distribute his work. Elite artists and an elite media industry are symbiotic. If you democratize media, then you end up democratizing talent. The unintended consequence of all this democratization, to misquote Web 2.0 apologist Thomas Friedman, is cultural "flattening." No more Hitchcocks, Bonos, or Sebalds. Just the flat noise of opinion—Socrates's nightmare.

The Dumbing Down of Web 2.0 Content

In ancient Greece, when fame was inextricably linked to posterity, an Alexander had to make his mark on history to insure that his praises would be sung by generations to come. . . . But the advent of cyberfame is remarkable in that it is divorced from any significant achievement—farting to the tune of "Jingle Bells," for example, can get you on VH1.

Lakshmi Chaudhry, "Mirror, Mirror on the Web," *Nation*, January 29, 2007.

An Overabundance of Art Is Nightmarish

While Socrates correctly gave warning about the dangers of a society infatuated by opinion in Plato's *Republic*, more modern dystopian writers—[Aldous] Huxley, [Ray] Bradbury, and [George] Orwell—got the Web 2.0 future exactly wrong. Much has been made for example, of the associations between the all-seeing, all-knowing qualities of Google's search engine and Big Brother in *Nineteen Eighty-Four*. But Orwell's fear was the disappearance of the individual right to self-expression. Thus [main character] Winston Smith's great act of rebellion in *Nineteen Eighty-Four* was his decision to pick up a rusty pen and express his own thoughts:

> The thing that he was about to do was open a diary. This was not illegal, but if detected it was reasonably certain that it would be punished by

The author argues that Web 2.0 gives an undeserved platform to amateur musicians, authors, filmmakers, and other untrained artists.

death. . . . Winston fitted a nib into the penholder and sucked it to get the grease off. . . . He dipped the pen into the ink and then faltered for just a second. A tremor had gone through his bowels. To mark the paper was the decisive act.

In the Web 2.0 world, however, the nightmare is not the scarcity, but the overabundance of authors. Since everyone will use digital media to express themselves, the only decisive act will be to not mark the paper. Not writing as rebellion sounds bizarre—like a piece of fiction authored by Franz Kafka. But one of the unintended consequences of the Web 2.0 future may well be that everyone is an author, while there is no longer any audience.

The Erosion of True Art

Speaking of Kafka, on the back cover of the January 2006 issue of *Poets and Writers* magazine, there is a seductive Web 2.0 style advertisement which reads:

Kafka toiled in obscurity and died penniless. If only he'd had a website. . . .

Presumably, if Kafka had had a website, it would be located at kafka.com which is today an address owned by a mad left-wing blog called The Biscuit Report. The front page of this site quotes some words written by Kafka in his diary:

I have no memory for things I have learned, nor things I have read, nor things experienced or heard, neither for people nor events; I feel that I have experienced nothing, learned nothing, that I actually know less than the average schoolboy, and that what I do know is superficial, and that every second question is beyond me. I am incapable of thinking deliberately; my thoughts run into a wall. I can grasp the essence of things in isolation, but I am quite incapable of coherent, unbroken thinking. I can't even tell a story properly; in fact, I can scarcely talk. . .

One of the unintended consequences of the Web 2.0 movement may well be that we fall, collectively, into the amnesia that Kafka describes. Without an elite mainstream media, we will lose our memory for things learnt, read, experienced, or heard. The cultural consequences of this are dire, requiring the authoritative voice of at least an Allan Bloom, if not an Oswald Spengler.[1] But here in Silicon Valley, on the brink of the Web 2.0 epoch, there no longer are any Blooms or Spenglers. All we have is the great seduction of citizen media, democratized content and authentic online communities. And weblogs, course. Millions and millions of blogs.

Analyze the essay:

1. Keen uses the term *democratization* to describe what Web 2.0 applications do to talent and media. Write one paragraph fleshing out his use of this term. Then state whether you think the democratization of talent and media is a positive or a negative thing, and why.

2. In this essay the author argues that Web 2.0 technologies level the artistic playing field, which results in the watering down of art and information. In the following essay Kevin Kelly argues that Web 2.0 technologies unleash a creative outpouring that results in even better content. After reading both essays, with which author do you ultimately agree, and why?

Web 2.0 Applications Result in Higher-Quality Information and Art

Kevin Kelly

Web 2.0 applications encourage people to create higher-quality information and art, argues Kevin Kelly in the following viewpoint, which was part of an e-mail exchange with Andrew Keen, author of the previous viewpoint. Kelly dismisses fears that technology that has put the tools of art in the hands of the masses will somehow water down the quality of what is created or cause art to become unprofitable. On the contrary, Kelly thinks such applications have inspired a creative outpouring the likes of which society has never seen. In his opinion, even if 90 percent of what is created is of poor quality, 10 percent of it will be great—and some of that will be better than what is produced by the media establishment. Kelly concludes that Web 2.0 applications allow art to be created and discovered not just by large studios or production companies but by audiences themselves.

Kevin Kelly cofounded *Wired* magazine in 1993 and served as its executive editor until 1999. He continues to write for *Wired*. He is the author of *Out of Control: The New Biology of Machines, Social Systems and the Economic World* and *New Rules for the New Economy*.

Consider the following questions:

1. How does the author think people fifty years from now will characterize the effect the Internet has had on art?
2. In what way did bad television result in the creation of fantastic television, according to Kelly?
3. What turned people from consumers into prosumers, according to the author?

Kevin Kelly, "The Internet Is Ninety Percent Amateur Crap: And Therein Lies Its Greatness," Jewcy.com, May 31, 2007. Reproduced by permission.

As I write this I am surrounded by my two-story library of tens of thousands of books, albums, magazines, catalogs, and photographic slides, which I have spent my life enjoying and which I plan to keep enjoying into the future. I don't need [American author] John Updike to remind me of the value and benefits of the old-fashioned paper book; I am in no hurry to see it go. But, more importantly, there's really nothing I can do to prevent its slow replacement by digital and hybrid versions.

In response to my "manifesto" [an article in which the author argued that digital technology will replace the printed book], Updike issued a wonderfully lyrical call for book lovers to build fortresses to keep out the wave of digital change. It was beautifully written, sweet, nostalgic, and of course totally inept, because it is clear that a tiny fort of book lovers cannot stop the oceanic change swamping the analog world. And I am enthusiastic about digital technology simply because I believe that in the end writers, readers, and publishers will gain more from the change than they lose.

More to Gain than to Lose

As new business models evolve, publishers/labels/studios will make more money—and more creative works—in this new regime than before. Everyone will benefit. Readers will have more choices in content. Authors/artists will have more opportunities to create than ever before. In 50 years people will marvel at all our hand-wringing and screams of bloody murder, because the creative outpouring that has just started online will produce a degree and volume of creative work that will dwarf the greatness of the last 50 years.

Will there be crap? Of course there will be. Ninety percent of everything made is crap. And that is good. One of the reasons TV went stagnant while online bloomed is that there was not enough bad—I mean really bad—TV. Television and movies cost so much to make and distribute that the system could not generate really, really bad

TV in the same way a web page, or even a book, can be really crap. Instead, the huge expense of producing TV and movies meant that the bad never had a chance. But neither did risky greatness, so all we got was mediocrity. We got middle-of-the-road TV, some shows better than others, but little of it either genius or total mind-numbing bad (and yes, I've seen daytime TV).

Out of Crap Comes High Quality

You don't know crap until you've trolled the depths of the web and self-publishing. But now with the advent of YouTube, digital-video tools, and cheap DVD rentals and sales, really bad TV has been liberated! And in the midst of this morass of total crap comes the freedom and risk to make really great TV. I think it's no coincidence that with the advent of the web, TV is now in its golden age. Shows like *Lost, 24, The Sopranos*, and *The Wire* will rank as this generation's greatest cultural contributions. They will be taught in university courses in centuries to come.

The greatness of these long-form TV shows was unleashed by the digital technology that made re-watching important, time-shifting easy, audience infatuation contagious, and new complexity totally engaging. They are produced by professionals with big budgets, and more shows like them will continue to be made and watched by large audiences. But shorter, amateur-made films will also reach the heights of greatness, now that the tyranny of the mediocre has been broken by really easy-to-make crap.

Transitions Are Always Rocky

Two admissions: one, we don't yet know how this bountiful new world will economically reward creators, and, two, the transition is likely to be ugly. The transition from the agricultural economy to the industrial was wracked with losses of livelihood, civil unrest, and bankruptcies, as well as fortunes and great uncertainty. Buggy whip–makers, who were real craftsmen, with real families, disappeared from the economy. Should we have stopped industrialization in order to save their jobs? Should we have stopped industrialization until we could explain to them how the new economy actually worked?

I believe a better remedy would have been to accept their occupation's demise and retrain them for their future. We can each make our own list of the sins of industrialization, but by our very participation in this industrialized world, we acknowledge that the benefits of industrialization were worth the loss of the beauty of an agricultural economy. Unless you are living like the Amish (which you can choose to do), you've voted for the costly advantages of industrialization. We are making a similar vote today with computer bits.

The web is all of 5,000 days old [as of 2007]. It may take another few thousand days to figure out viable systems of law, business practices, and cultural norms that will reward audiences, creators, and the middle industries. Or it may take a generation. But that is still a relatively short time in the lifecycle of an economy.

Art Will Continue to Be Profitable

What's the evidence that these new models will come? My expectations are largely the product of my own experience. While I am a published author, with commercial books still in print generating royalties, the majority of my income does not come from paper books. It comes from a plurality of sources: syndication rights, speaking fees, online advertising, direct digital sales, and associative marketing revenues on the web. Am I an exception? I don't think so. The one thing I've learned is that whenever I think I am an exception, it turns out that I am only a little early and the rest of the world will soon be there to make it clear my ideas are not mine. My pattern will be ordinary.

The principle that will ensure an income for the world's artists and publishers, bands and labels, is that wherever attention flows, money will follow. If you are able to sustain the attention of an audience, and keep them interested over time, then money will flow to you. It will come both directly and indirectly (ads, sponsorship, middle folk),

> ### More Information Advances Society
>
> Never before has so much information about so many topics been so readily available to the general population of the earth. This level of intellectual proliferation is unprecedented in human history, and it will only contribute to the most profound event of cultural diffusion our species has ever known, thereby increasing not only the general education of mankind but also, by consequence, raising the global standard of living.
>
> Geoffrey Greer, "In Defense of Wikipedia and Other Digital Media," *The Public Servant*, April 29, 2010.

Web 2.0 Is Just the Beginning

Web 2.0 applications are already giving way to what are called Web 3.0 applications, which expand upon older technologies and allow users to do even more.

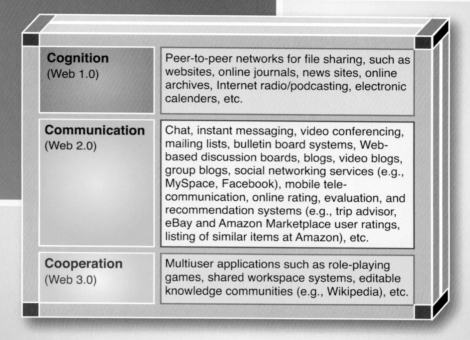

Cognition (Web 1.0)	Peer-to-peer networks for file sharing, such as websites, online journals, news sites, online archives, Internet radio/podcasting, electronic calenders, etc.
Communication (Web 2.0)	Chat, instant messaging, video conferencing, mailing lists, bulletin board systems, Web-based discussion boards, blogs, video blogs, group blogs, social networking services (e.g., MySpace, Facebook), mobile tele-communication, online rating, evaluation, and recommendation systems (e.g., trip advisor, eBay and Amazon Marketplace user ratings, listing of similar items at Amazon), etc.
Cooperation (Web 3.0)	Multiuser applications such as role-playing games, shared workspace systems, editable knowledge communities (e.g., Wikipedia), etc.

Taken from: Christian Fuehs, *Social Networking Sites and the Surveillance Society. Salzburg and Vienna, Austria:* Research Group Unified Theory of Information, 2009, p.7.

but it will come for two reasons. One, because we are bored and will pay for something that elevates us above life's averageness, and, two, because we crave to connect with creators who elevate and equip us. We want to pay; just make paying easy, just, and beneficial.

More Art, Rather than the Death of Art

The funny thing about the supposed demise of high culture (authors and books, musicians and music, directors and films) supported by classic industrial economics is that we see the demise everywhere except in the statistics. There are more books, songs, films, etc., being made every year, and more artists, authors, and musicians working than ever before. Every bit of data I have been able to find points to yet more artists and more art in the coming years. It could be that this outpouring is a heroic last gasp before culture's ultimate disappearance by digital technology, but I doubt it. Far more likely is that this outpouring is due to the peculiar and nearly metaphysical properties of digital technology, which has turned many millions of consumers into *pro*sumers.

You can call them amateurs, but I call them a miracle. During the 1980s and even into the early '90s, I struggled to convince the heads of media companies that the participatory nature of the Internet was real. They were convinced that online enthusiasts like myself were exceptions. The Internet was a young male domain, they insisted, that would not appeal to females, anyone older than 19, or those living in the heartland. They were even more adamant that "no one would ever get up from the couch to make their own videos," let alone write text. The idea of millions of videos being made by the audience was absolutely unthinkable. It was impossible. My own experiences living online, prosuming media with many others, were declared an aberrant exception. My vision of a billion people owning computers, actively creating text, videos, and music in some kind of online network was dismissed as raving utopianism.

If 90 Percent Is Crap, 10 Percent Is Greatness

Who can argue against the goodness of having a billion people get off the couches and start making stuff, even if 90 percent is crap? That means 10 percent is great. And not only is that 10 percent more than we had before, I will argue that eventually some of that 10 percent will be superior to the best we get from the established media industry. And even if the greatest is never made by prosumers, it is still wonderful they are off their butts and using the talents that God gave them.

Analyze the essay:

1. In this essay Kelly uses history, facts, examples, and persuasive reasoning to make his argument that Web 2.0 applications enhance the quality of art and information. He does not, however, use any quotations to support his point. If you were to rewrite this article and insert quotations, what authorities might you quote from? Where would you place these quotations to bolster the points Kelly makes?

2. Kelly reminds readers that the Web is a very young technology—about five thousand days old as of 2007—and it is reasonable to expect it to take a while to work out its kinks. Imagine what the Internet might look like in another five thousand days. What might Web 2.0 applications have evolved to by then? How might art and information be affected by the Web of the future? Write two to three paragraphs on what this future Internet might be like and use persuasive techniques to convince your reader to agree with you.

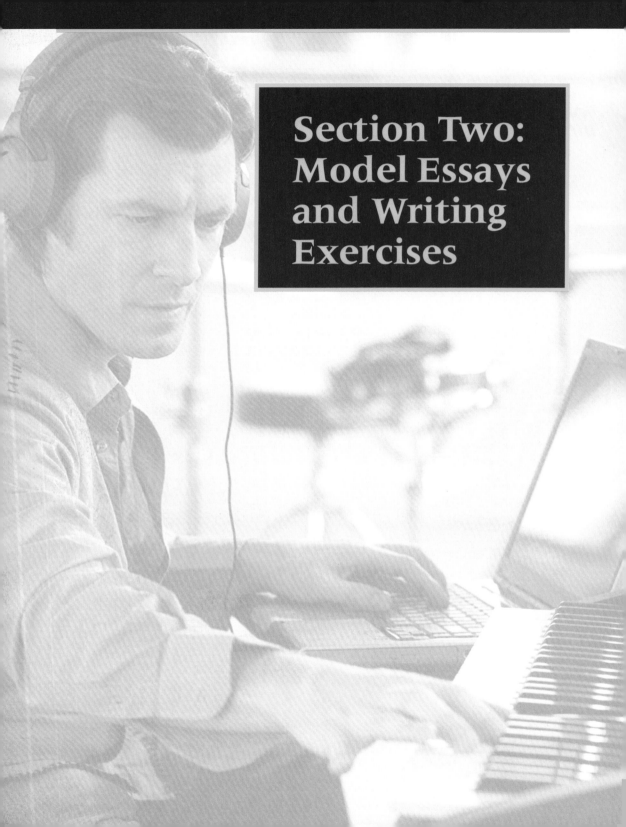

Section Two: Model Essays and Writing Exercises

The Five-Paragraph Essay

An *essay* is a short piece of writing that discusses or analyzes one topic. The five-paragraph essay is a form commonly used in school assignments and tests. Every five-paragraph essay begins with an *introduction*, ends with a *conclusion*, and features three *supporting paragraphs* in the middle.

The Thesis Statement. The introduction includes the essay's thesis statement. The thesis statement presents the argument or point the author is trying to make about the topic. The essays in this book all have different thesis statements because they are making different arguments about Web 2.0 applications.

The thesis statement should clearly tell the reader what the essay will be about. A focused thesis statement helps determine what will be in the essay; the subsequent paragraphs are spent developing and supporting its argument.

The Introduction. In addition to presenting the thesis statement, a well-written introductory paragraph captures the attention of the reader and explains why the topic being explored is important. It may provide the reader with background information on the subject matter or feature an anecdote that illustrates a point relevant to the topic. It could also present startling information that clarifies the point of the essay or put forth a contradictory position that the essay will refute. Further techniques for writing an introduction are found later in this section.

The Supporting Paragraphs. The introduction is then followed by three (or more) supporting paragraphs. These are the main body of the essay. Each paragraph presents and develops a *subtopic* that supports the essay's thesis statement. Each subtopic is spearheaded by a *topic sentence* and supported by its own facts, details, and examples. The writer can use various kinds of supporting material and details to back up the topic of each supporting paragraph. These may include statistics, quotations from people with special knowledge or expertise, historic facts, and anecdotes. A rule of writing is that specific and concrete examples are more convincing than vague, general, or unsupported assertions.

The Conclusion. The conclusion is the paragraph that closes the essay. Its function is to summarize or reiterate the main idea of the essay. It may recall an idea from the introduction or briefly examine the larger implications of the thesis. Because the conclusion is also the last chance a writer has to make an impression on the reader, it is important that it not simply repeat what has been presented elsewhere in the essay but close it in a clear, final, and memorable way.

Although the order of the essay's component paragraphs is important, they do not have to be written in the order presented here. Some writers like to decide on a thesis and write the introduction paragraph first. Other writers like to focus first on the body of the essay, and write the introduction and conclusion later.

Pitfalls to Avoid

When writing essays about controversial issues such as the Internet and social media, it is important to remember that disputes over the material are common precisely because there are many different perspectives. Remember to state your arguments in careful and measured terms. Evaluate your topic fairly—avoid overstating negative qualities of one perspective or understating positive qualities of another. Use examples, facts, and details to support any assertions you make.

The Persuasive Essay

There are many types of essays, but in general, they are usually short compositions in which the writer expresses and discusses an opinion about something. In the persuasive essay the writer tries to persuade (convince) the reader to do something or to agree with the writer's opinion about something. Examples of persuasive writing are easy to find. Advertising is one common example. Through commercial and print ads, companies try to convince the public to buy their products for specific reasons. A lot of everyday writing is persuasive, too. Letters to the editor, posts from sports fans on team websites, even handwritten notes urging a friend to listen to a new CD—all are examples of persuasive writing.

The Tools of Persuasion

The writer of the persuasive essay uses various tools to persuade the reader. Here are some of them:

Facts and Statistics. A fact is a statement that no one, typically, would disagree with. It can be verified by information in reputable resources, such as encyclopedias, almanacs, government websites, or reference books about the topic of the fact.

Examples of Facts and Statistics

New Year's Eve is celebrated on December 31.
Tokyo is the capital of Japan.
Twenty percent of all pregnancies end in miscarriage.
According to the National Center for Education
    Statistics, 32 percent of students aged twelve to
    eighteen report being involved in bullying as
    a bully, a target of bullying, or both.

It is important to note that facts and statistics can be *misstated* (written down or quoted incorrectly), *misinterpreted* (not understood correctly by the user), or *misused* (not used fairly). But if a writer uses facts and statistics properly, they can add authority to the writer's essay.

Opinions. An opinion is what a person thinks about something. It can be contested or argued with. However, opinions of people who are experts on the topic or who have personal experience are often very convincing. Many persuasive essays are written to convince the reader that the writer's opinion is worth believing and acting on.

Testimonials. A testimonial is a statement given by a person who is thought to be an expert or who has another trait people admire, such as being a celebrity. Television commercials frequently use testimonials to convince watchers to buy the products they are advertising.

Examples. An example is something that is representative of a group or type: Rotini is an example of the type of food known as pasta. Examples are used to help define, describe, or illustrate something to make it more understandable.

Anecdotes. Anecdotes are extended examples. They are little stories with a beginning, middle, and end. They can be used just like examples to explain something or to show something about a topic.

Appeals to Reason. One way to convince readers that an opinion or action is right is to appeal to reason or logic. This often involves the idea that if some ideas are true, another must also be true. Here is an example of one type of appeal to reason:

— Eating fast food causes obesity and diabetes, just as smoking cigarettes causes lung cancer and asthma. For this reason, fast food companies, like cigarette manufacturers, should be held legally responsible for their customers' health.

Appeals to Emotion. Another way to persuade readers to believe or do something is to appeal to their emotions— love, fear, pity, loyalty, and anger are some of the emotions to which writers appeal. A writer who wants to persuade someone not to eat meat might appeal to their love of animals:

— If you own a cat, dog, hamster, or bird, you should not eat meat. It makes no sense to pamper and love your pet while at the same time supporting the merciless slaughter of other animals for your dinner.

Ridicule and Name-Calling. Ridicule and name-calling are not good techniques to use in a persuasive essay. Instead of exploring the strengths of the topic, the writer who uses these relies on making those who oppose the main idea look foolish, evil, or stupid. In most cases, the writer who does this weakens his or her argument.

Bandwagon. The writer who uses the bandwagon technique uses the idea that "everybody thinks this or is doing this; therefore it is valid." The bandwagon method is not a very authoritative way to convince your reader of your point.

Words and Phrases Common to Persuasive Essays

accordingly	it stands to reason
because	it then follows that
clearly	obviously
consequently	since
for this reason	subsequently
indeed	therefore
it is necessary to	this is why
it makes sense to	thus
it seems clear that	we must

Antisocial Networking: How Facebook Is Hurting Your Friendships

Editor's Notes Persuasive essays commonly attempt to persuade a reader to agree that there is a specific reason or cause for a problem. This is the goal of the following model essay. It argues that social networking sites devalue friendship. The author offers three reasons for why she thinks that social networking sites do not enhance—and even erode—personal relationships. The essay is structured as a five-paragraph essay in which each paragraph contributes a supporting piece of evidence to develop the argument.

The notes in the margin point out key features of the essay and will help you understand how the essay is organized. Also note that all sources are cited using Modern Language Association (MLA) style.* For more information on how to cite your sources, see Appendix C. In addition, consider the following:

1. How does the introduction engage the reader's attention?
2. What persuasive techniques are used in the essay?
3. What purpose do the essay's quotes serve?
4. Does the essay convince you of its point?

Refers to thesis and topic sentences

Refers to supporting details

Paragraph 1

This is the essay's thesis statement. It tells the reader what will be argued in the following paragraphs.

Eons, BlackPlanet, MySpace, LinkedIn, Facebook—these are just a few of the more than fifty social networking sites that claim to bring people closer together, no matter where they live and work. But in reality such sites do

---

* Editor's Note: In applying MLA style guidelines in this book, the following simplifications have been made: Parenthetical text citations are confined to direct quotations only; electronic source documentation in the Works Cited list omits date of access, page ranges, and some detailed facts of publication.

nothing to enhance existing relationships and fail to create any meaningful new ones. The best thing we can do for our friendships is to close the accounts we have on these *anti*social networking sites and work to cultivate our friendships in face-to-face settings.

Paragraph 2

True friendships are made up primarily of intimate in-person interactions marked by laughter, conversation, shared experiences and activities, and, occasionally, a mutual tear—none of these, however, can be obtained via social networking sites. Rather, such sites devalue friendship by promoting a shortcut approach to friendship. The personal investment that is required to forge and maintain a close friendship cannot be replicated by the instant gratification, click-and-befriend nature of the social networking format. "Having been relegated to our screens, are our friendships now anything more than a form of distraction?" asks one writer. "When they've shrunk to the size of a wall post, do they retain any content? If we have 768 'friends,' in what sense do we have any?" (Deresiewicz) Indeed, true friendships take so much work that it is impossible to have more than a handful of truly meaningful ones at any one time, let alone the dozens, even hundreds, claimed on social networking sites.

This is the topic sentence of Paragraph 2. It is a subset of the essay's thesis that tells what specific point this paragraph will be about.

"Rather" and "indeed" are transitional words. They keep the thoughts linked and the ideas moving.

This quote was taken from the box accompanying Viewpoint Two. This book is filled with many useful quotes and facts you can use in your own essay.

Paragraph 3

Social media users themselves say that social networking sites have not deepened or strengthened their relationships. According to a 2010 study by Red Associates, a Denmark-based polling company, 90 percent of Facebook users interviewed said that when they first created their Facebook account, they expected their use of the site to "deepen or strengthen their friendships." In reality, however, more than half said they use Facebook as a way to manage their relationships without meaningfully deepening them. Furthermore, just 0.7 percent of respondents said that Facebook's main benefit was to strengthen friendships. In addition, 40 percent of respondents added

This is the topic sentence of Paragraph 3. Without reading the rest of the paragraph, take a guess at what the paragraph will be about.

friends not because they shared a meaningful connection with a person, but because it was "easy" to do so. "Online social networks make it easy for people to accumulate friends rapidly and to make commitments easily," said the Red Associates study authors. "What define[s] social networks most [is] a *lack* of depth in relationships." (Qtd. in Carr) Making things worse is the fact that once on a site like Facebook, people rarely use their account to enhance their relationships. Rather, status updates, photo comments, or other pithy uses of their account become a poor substitute for telephone, in-person, or even substantive e-mail contact that they previously had with friends.

Paragraph 4

Perhaps most telling is the fact that the generation coming of age immersed in this friendship-promoting technology is worse off for it: psychiatrists have noticed that teenagers born since 1990—those who have never known a world without the Internet—are increasingly unable to form lasting, meaningful friendships and are more likely to take friendship for granted. As British psychiatrist Himanshu Tyagi has put it, the Web 2.0 universe is "a world where everything moves fast and changes all the time, where relationships are quickly disposed at the click of a mouse, where you can delete your profile if you don't like it and swap an unacceptable identity in the blink of an eye for one that is more acceptable." (Qtd. in Smith) Such sites have taught young people that friendships can be created—and ended—in a matter of moments, which is neither a true nor healthy outlook. Young people need to know that true friendships are not developed by throwing a sheep at one another or by sending each other a cartoon martini.

Paragraph 5

Social networking sites are not entirely a waste of time—when supported by real-life interactions they can be a useful way for busy friends to keep tabs on each other. But when the bulk of our social interactions end up taking place online, it's a clear signal to close the computer and pick up an older technology—the good old phone. To prevent your friendships from being reduced to a superficial mockery, close your Facebook account today.

Works Cited

Carr, Austin, "Users of Facebook's Social Network Are Mostly Anti-Social: Poll." *Fast Company* 5 May 2010. < http://www.fastcompany.com/1638333/shocker-users-of-facebooks-social-network-are-mostly-anti-social > .

Deresiewicz, William, "Faux Friendship." *Chronicle of Higher Education* 6 Dec. 2009. < http://chronicle.com/article/Faux-Friendship/49308/ > .

Smith, Rebecca, "Facebook and MySpace Generation 'Cannot Form Lasting Relationships.'" *Daily Telegraph* (London) 3 Jul. 2008. < http://www.telegraph.co.uk/technology/3357741/Facebook-and-MySpace-generation-cannot-form-relationships.html > .

Exercise 1A: Create an Outline from an Existing Essay

It often helps to create an outline of the five-paragraph essay before you write it. The outline can help you organize the information, arguments, and evidence you have gathered during your research.

For this exercise, create an outline that could have been used to write "Antisocial Networking: How Facebook Is Hurting Your Friendships." This "reverse engineering" exercise is meant to help familiarize you with how outlines can help classify and arrange information.

To do this you will need to
1. articulate the essay's thesis,
2. pinpoint important pieces of evidence,
3. flag quotes that supported the essay's ideas, and
4. identify key points that support the argument.

Part of the outline has already been started to give you an idea of the assignment.

Outline
I. Paragraph 1
Write the essay's thesis:

II. Paragraph 2
Topic: Real friendships are made up primarily of intimate face-to-face interactions not available on social networking sites.
　　Supporting Detail i.

　　Supporting Detail ii. True friendships take so much work that it is impossible to have more than a handful of truly meaningful ones at any one time.

III. Paragraph 3
Topic:

   Supporting Detail i. Statistics from Red Associates showing that Facebook users do not think their use of the site has enhanced their friendships.
   Supporting Detail ii.

IV. Paragraph 4
Topic:

   Supporting Detail i. Quote from British psychiatrist Himanshu Tyagi
   Supporting Detail ii.

V. Paragraph 5
Write the essay's conclusion:

Exercise 1B: Create an Outline for Your Own Essay

The model essay you just read expresses a particular point of view about social networking. For this exercise, your assignment is to find supporting ideas, choose specific and concrete details, create an outline, and ultimately write a five-paragraph essay making a different, or even opposing, point about social networking. Your goal is to use persuasive techniques to convince your reader.

Part 1: Write a thesis statement.

The following thesis statement would be appropriate for an opposing essay arguing that social networking sites enhance friendships:

Social networking sites allow friends to have a valuable window into each other's day-to-day lives—Facebook might singlehandedly abolish the concept of being "out of the loop" or needing to "catch up."

Or see the sample paper topics suggested in Appendix D for more ideas.

Part II: Brainstorm pieces of supporting evidence.

Using information from some of the viewpoints in the previous section and from the information found in Section Three of this book, write down three arguments or pieces of evidence that support the thesis statement you selected. Then, for each of these three arguments, write down supportive facts, examples, and details that support it. These could be:

- statistical information;
- personal memories and anecdotes;
- quotes from experts, peers, or family member;
- observations of people's actions and behaviors;
- specific and concrete details.

Supporting pieces of evidence for the above sample thesis statement are found in this book and include:

- Quote from Viewpoint One by Jessica Misener about how Facebook facilitates real-life interactions: "Through Facebook, I've received party invitations, heard about high school reunion plans and found out that scores of my friends of yesteryear have relocated to New York, making it easy for us to meet up."
- Chart accompanying Viewpoint One that shows that millions of people use social networking sites, indicating that they find social value in them.

- Quote in the box accompanying Viewpoint One by Karen Goldberg Goff that shows that social networking sites decrease isolation: "While the majority of teens use sites such as MySpace and Facebook to hang out with people they already know in real life, a smaller portion uses them to find like-minded people. Before social networking, the one kid in school who was, say, a fan of Godzilla or progressive politics might find himself isolated. These days, that youngster has peers everywhere." For the whole article, see Karen Goldberg Goff, "Social Networking Benefits Validated," *Washington Times*, January 28, 2009.

Part III: Place the information from Part I in outline form.

Part IV: Write the arguments or supporting statements in paragraph form.

By now you have three arguments that support the paragraph's thesis statement, as well as supporting material. Use the outline to write out your three supporting arguments in paragraph form. Make sure each paragraph has a topic sentence that states the paragraph's thesis clearly and broadly. Then, add supporting sentences that express the facts, quotes, details, and examples that support the paragraph's argument. The paragraph may also have a concluding or summary sentence.

Citizen Journalists Are Killing the News

Editor's Notes The following model essay argues that citizen journalists share the blame for the struggles of newspapers and professional journalists. Like the first model essay, this essay is structured as a five-paragraph persuasive essay in which each paragraph contributes a supporting piece of evidence to develop the argument. Each supporting paragraph explores one of three distinct reasons why the author thinks that citizen journalists are no substitute for professional journalists.

As you read this essay, take note of its components and how they are organized (the sidebars in the margins provide further explanation).

Paragraph 1

The news industry is at death's door: Since 2007, more than 180 newspapers have closed or stopped publishing a print edition, which has resulted in the loss of more than thirty-four thousand jobs. While lack of revenue and lack of interest in print news is partly to blame for the decline, some of it can be attributed to the rise in the number of bloggers and citizen journalists, regular people who take it upon themselves to report on newsworthy events in their community. The rise of citizen journalism is a dangerous and stupid fad that threatens to undermine one of the most important and long-standing American institutions: the free press.

What is the essay's thesis statement? How did you recognize it?

Paragraph 2

Our society depends on professionally trained journalists to break important stories, uncover corporate and government scandals, and distribute critical information that keeps multiple sectors of society in check. Yet citizen journalists are not trained professionals, have few or no

72

resources and credentials at their disposal, and work with no budget. It seems obvious, then, that they are incapable of delivering the hard-hitting, investigative journalism that is so critical to the functioning of a democratic society. As David Simon, a former writer for the *Baltimore Sun* and creator of the HBO series *The Wire*, has put it, "I am offended to think that anyone, anywhere believes that American institutions as insulated, self-preserving, and self-justifying as police departments, school systems, legislatures, and chief executives can be held to [account] . . . by amateurs, pursuing the task without compensation, training, or for that matter, sufficient standing to make public officials even care to whom it is they are lying or from whom they are withholding information." (Qtd. in Hogg) As former Washington Post writer Neil Henry has pointed out, there will be no shortage of scandals to break, but there will be a shortage of qualified journalists to uncover them.

Identify a piece of evidence used to support Paragraph 2's main idea.

The author has paraphrased Neil Henry, author of Viewpoint Three. For more on paraphrasing, see Appendix B in this book.

Paragraph 3

In addition, because citizen journalists are not professionally trained writers, their stories are prone to error. Bloggers and iReporters are under no obligation to check facts, verify sources, or even write well. One study conducted by the Pew Internet & American Life Project found that 34 percent of bloggers consider their posts to be a form of journalism. Yet only about the same number—about 33 percent—said that they verify facts, link to source material, or conduct other journalistic tasks. The stories these people produce, therefore, are likely to be laden with mistakes, both factual and grammatical. An excellent example of the error-prone citizen journalist is James O'Keefe, the investigative undercover reporter who in 2009 made controversial videos of the community organizing group ACORN and, in 2010, of government census workers. While his videos brought problems with both organizations to light, O'Keefe made incorrect assumptions, used fuzzy logic, and employed potentially illegal investigative methods that made his "work" easy to discount. Professional journalists, on the other hand, hold

This is the topic sentence of Paragraph 3. Note that all of the paragraph's details support it.

What transitional words and phrases are used in the essay? Make a list of all that appear.

bachelor's and master's degrees in their field and typically have years of on-the-job training that helps them to ask hard-hitting questions, properly vet their sources, and accurately confirm their information. "The fact is there will be nothing on YouTube, or in the blogosphere, or anywhere else on the Web to effectively replace the valuable work of those professionals." (Henry)

Paragraph 4

Finally, citizen journalists tend to write short, pithy, opinion-laden blurbs. But to stay informed, the public needs to read detailed, objective, and substantial reports. As one news editor has put it, "Just imagine how uninformed the public will be when news reports are as brief and trivial as a Facebook comment." (Sheppard) Indeed, most bloggers' posts are short because they have nothing of real value to say. We must encourage real journalism that treats news seriously and comprehensively, and eschew the kind of superficial writing that comprises the average blog post.

What do you think made the author want to include this quote? There are two reasons.

Paragraph 5

Citizen journalists can make important contributions to rapidly breaking stories—when a natural or human-made disaster strikes, for example, citizen journalists are often on the scene faster than the traditional news media and are thus in a unique position to take critical photographs or describe the fast-changing incident. But when it comes to serious news, we continue to need the expertise of professional journalists. We must protect this vital institution by letting journalists do their job and keeping untrained and unqualified citizens in their rightful place.

Works Cited

Henry, Neil. "The Decline of News." *San Francisco Chronicle* 29 May 2007, B5. < http://articles.sfgate.com/2007-05-29/opinion/17244065_1_chronicle-online-advertising-journalists > .

Hogg, Chris. "Did the Internet Kill Journalism?" *Digital Journal* 11 May 2009. <www.digitaljournal.com/article/271696>.

Sheppard, Noel. "Will Social Networking Sites Like Facebook Destroy Our Society?" NewsBusters 25 Aug. 2009. <http://newsbusters.org/blogs/noel-sheppard/2009/08/25/will-social-networking-sites-facebook-destroy-society#ixzz0dlIWadJm>.

Exercise 2A: Create an Outline from an Existing Essay

As you did for the first model essay in this section, create an outline that could have been used to write "Citizen Journalists Are Killing the News." Be sure to identify the essay's thesis statement, its supporting ideas and details, and key pieces of evidence that were used.

Exercise 2B: Identify Persuasive Techniques

Essayists use many techniques to get you to agree with their ideas or to do something they want you to do. Some of the most common techniques are described in Preface B of this section, "The Persuasive Essay." These tools are *facts* and *statistics, opinions, testimonials, examples* and *anecdotes, appeals to reason, appeals to emotion, ridicule* and *name-calling,* and *bandwagon.* Go back to the preface and review these tools. Remember that most of these tools can be used to enhance your essay, but some of them—particularly ridicule, name-calling, and bandwagon—can detract from the essay's effectiveness. Nevertheless, you should be able to recognize them in the essays you read.

Some writers use one persuasive tool throughout their whole essay. For example, the essay may be one extended anecdote, or the writer may rely entirely on statistics. But most writers typically use a combination of persuasive tools. Essay Two, "Citizen Journalists Are Killing the News," does this.

Problem One
Read Essay Two again and see if you can find every persuasive tool used. Put that information in the following table. Part of the table is filled in for you. Explanatory notes are below the table. (NOTE: You will not fill in every box. No paragraph contains all of the techniques.)

	Paragraph 1 Sentence #	Paragraph 2 Sentence #	Paragraph 3 Sentence #	Paragraph 4 Sentence #	Paragraph 5 Sentence #
Fact	1[a]				
Statistic			3[c]		
Opinion		3[b]			
Testimonial					
Example			6 and 7[d]		
Anecdote					
Appeal to Reason					
Appeal to Emotion					
Ridicule				4[e]	
Name-Calling					
Bandwagon					

Notes
a. It is a *fact* that since 2007, more than 180 newspapers have closed or stopped publishing a print edition, which has resulted in the loss of more than thirty-four thousand jobs.
b. It is the author's *opinion* that citizen journalists are incapable of delivering hard-hitting, investigative journalism.
c. That 34 percent of bloggers consider their posts a form of journalism is a *statistic*.
d. James O'Keefe is an example of how the work of citizen journalists is unprofessional.
e. When the author says, "most bloggers' posts are short because they have nothing of real value to say," she is *ridiculing* them.

Now, look at the table you have produced. Which persuasive tools does this essay rely on most heavily? Which are not used at all?

Problem Two
Apply this exercise to the other model essays in this section and to the viewpoints in Section One when you are finished reading them.

The Political Power of Social Networking

Editor's Notes The final model essay argues that social networking and Web 2.0 applications play a powerful role in national elections. Supported by facts, quotes, statistics, and opinions, it tries to persuade the reader that websites such as Facebook and Twitter have shaped national elections in both the United States and Iran and should therefore be regarded as powerful technologies.

This essay differs from the previous model essays in that it is longer than five paragraphs. Sometimes five paragraphs are simply not enough to develop an idea adequately. Extending the length of an essay can allow the reader to explore a topic in more depth or present multiple pieces of evidence that together provide a complete picture of a topic. Longer essays can also help readers discover the complexity of a subject by examining a topic beyond its superficial exterior. Moreover, the ability to write a sustained research or position paper is a valuable skill you will need as you advance academically.

As you read, consider the questions posed in the margins. Continue to identify thesis statements, supporting details, transitions, and quotations. Examine the introductory and concluding paragraphs to understand how they give shape to the essay. Finally, evaluate the essay's general structure and assess its overall effectiveness.

Paragraph 1

What is the essay's thesis statement? How did you recognize it?

Most people with a Facebook account use it to post pictures of their pet or play FarmVille. They use Twitter to update others on mundane events, such as what flavor smoothie they just ordered at the corner deli. But Facebook, Twitter, and other social networking sites have occasionally been used for more serious purposes, such as influencing the outcome of a national election or reporting on a revolution in the making. Two recent events demonstrate the political power of social networking services and indicate the significance that these media are likely to take on in the future.

Paragraph 2

During the 2008 presidential campaign, Barack Obama made masterly use of social networking platforms to electrify voters and catapult himself to the presidency. Researcher Paul van Veenendaal reports that during the campaign, Obama used more than fifteen social networking sites—including MySpace, Facebook, BlackPlanet (a social networking site for African Americans), and Eons (a Facebook-style site for Americans in their fifties and sixties)—to gain more than 5 million supporters. On Facebook alone, 3.2 million people joined his profile page. Since he has become president, more than 8 million have linked to him on Facebook and more than 4 million people follow him on Twitter.

Paragraph 3

Obama used the power of social networking to make his campaign seem active and current. He did not merely establish profiles at social networking sites—he vigorously used them to engage his supporters in dialogue and inspire them to act on his behalf. During the campaign he and his staffers wrote more than four hundred thousand blog posts. These in turn sparked the creation of more than thirty-five thousand groups of people who volunteered around the country on his behalf. These volunteers sponsored at least two hundred thousand events. This intense interest in—and ultimate election of—Obama stemmed directly from his use of social networking media. "The Obama campaign did not invent anything completely new," writes *New York Times* reporter David Carr. "Instead, by bolting together social networking applications under the banner of a movement, they created an unforeseen force to raise money, organize locally, fight smear campaigns and get out the vote."

> What is the topic sentence of Paragraph 3? How did you recognize it?

Paragraph 4

In addition to using existing social networking sites, Obama created his own. During the campaign, my.barack obama.com registered more than 2 million people who created profiles in support of the politician. In engaging these supporters, Obama got more than just their support—he also collected their contact information, which became a valuable tool once he was in office. "When he arrives at 1600 Pennsylvania, Mr. Obama will have not just a political base, but a database, millions of names of supporters who can be engaged almost instantly. And there's every reason to believe that he will use the network not just to campaign, but to govern." (Carr)

What transitional words and phrases are used in the essay? Make a list.

Paragraph 5

Lawyer and blogger Ranjit Mathoda points out that Obama is part of a select group of influential politicians who have embraced the technology of their day in a unique and visionary way. "Thomas Jefferson used newspapers to win the presidency, F.D.R. [Franklin Delano Roosevelt] used radio to change the way he governed, J.F.K. [John F. Kennedy] was the first president to understand television, and [2004 Democratic presidential hopeful] Howard Dean saw the value of the Web for raising money," says Mathoda. "But Senator Barack Obama understood that you could use the Web to lower the cost of building a political brand, create a sense of connection and engagement, and dispense with the command and control method of governing to allow people to self-organize to do the work." (Qtd. in Carr) Indeed, Obama's visionary use of social networking applications secured him the presidency and established him as a twenty-first-century Web-savvy politician.

Identify a piece of evidence used to support Paragraph 5's main idea.

Paragraph 6

A year after social networking helped Obama get elected in the United States, it played an important role in another election halfway around the world: the 2009 Iranian election. The June 12 elections in that country generated controversy when it seemed clear that the incumbent president, Mahmoud Ahmedinejad, had rigged the election to defeat his popular opponent, Mir Hossein Mousavi. After Ahmedinejad's victory was announced, people took to the streets en masse to protest, and a massive government crackdown followed. Trying to stem the opposition to its hold on power, the Iranian government censored almost all media forms, including newspapers and websites.

What experts or organizations are quoted in the essay? Make a list of everyone quoted, along with their credentials.

Paragraph 7

In the wake of the crackdown, very little information about the protests got out through mainstream media sources. But protesters were able to use Twitter to send out, or tweet, information about what was happening on the ground. Although the government could censor static websites, it could not shut down Twitter because of the way it broadcasts publicly and over a short message service, rather than Internet, medium. "While the front pages of Iranian newspapers were full of blank space where censors had whited-out news stories, Twitter was delivering information from street level, in real time," writes reporter Lev Grossman. Indeed, that it is easy to use, fast-spreading, and free "makes Twitter practically ideal for a mass protest movement, both very easy for the average citizen to use and very hard for any central authority to control." (Grossman) Reporter Noam Cohen agrees: "Twitter . . . prove[d] to be a crucial tool in the cat-and-mouse game between the opposition and the government over enlisting world opinion. As the Iranian government restricts journalists' access to events, the protesters have used Twitter's agile communication system to direct the public and journalists alike to video, photographs and written material related to the protests."

What point does this quote directly support?

Paragraph 8

With no other way to get their message out, Twitter users told the world about how government agents were aggressively—even violently—treating protesters. *"Woman says ppl knocking on her door 2 AM saying they*

What is the topic sentence of Paragraph 8? What pieces of evidence are used to show it is true?

What tools of persuasion have been used thus far in the essay? See Preface B and Exercise 2B in this section for more information on persuasive techniques.

were intelligence agents, took her daughter," tweeted one user. *"We hear 1 dead in* [the city of] *shiraz, livefire used in other cities,"* wrote another. (Qtd. in Grossman) In addition to being the best way to communicate, tweets were also broadcast in real time, giving the events in Iran a real-life immediacy that traditional news reports often lack. Individually the tweets were not always significant, but taken together they painted a picture of a popular uprising under fire by a government trying desperately to hold on to power. According to Cohen, this is what is significant about the medium: "Each update may not be important. Collectively, however, the tweets can create a personality or environment that reflects the emotions of the moment and helps drive opinion."

Paragraph 9

Although social networking and Web 2.0 applications are primarily used for social or even silly purposes, they are increasingly being used for serious political issues. As the technology continues to change and grow, one can expect sites like Twitter and Facebook to play an even more important role in groundbreaking political and social events.

Works Cited

Carr, David. "How Obama Tapped into Social Networks' Power." *New York Times* 9 Nov., 2008: B1.

Cohen, Noam. "Twitter on the Barricades: Six Lessons Learned." *New York Times* 20 Jun., 2009.

Grossman, Lev. "Twitter, the Medium of the Movement." *Time* 17 Jun., 2009.

Exercise 3A: Examining Introductions and Conclusions

Every essay features introductory and concluding paragraphs that are used to frame the main ideas being presented. Along with presenting the essay's thesis statement, well-written introductions should grab the attention of the reader and make clear why the topic being explored is important. The conclusion reiterates the essay's thesis and is also the last chance for the writer to make an impression on the reader. Strong introductions and conclusions can greatly enhance an essay's effect on an audience.

The Introduction

There are several techniques that can be used to craft an introductory paragraph. An essay can start with:

- an anecdote: a brief story that illustrates a point relevant to the topic;
- startling information: facts or statistics that elucidate the point of the essay;
- setting up and knocking down a position: a position or claim believed by proponents of one side of a controversy, followed by statements that challenge that claim;
- historical perspective: an example of the way things used to be that leads into a discussion of how or why things work differently now;
- summary information: general introductory information about the topic that feeds into the essay's thesis statement.

1. Reread the introductory paragraphs of the model essays and of the viewpoints in Section One. Identify which techniques described above are used in the example essays. How do they grab the attention of the reader? Are their thesis statements clearly presented?
2. Write an introduction for the essay you have outlined and partially written in Exercise 1B using one of the techniques described above.

The Conclusion

The conclusion brings the essay to a close by summarizing or returning to its main ideas. Good conclusions, however, go beyond simply repeating these ideas. Strong conclusions explore a topic's broader implications and reiterate why it is important to consider. They may frame the essay by returning to an anecdote featured in the opening paragraph. Or they may close with a quotation or refer back to an event in the essay. In opinionated essays, the conclusion can reiterate which side the essay is taking or ask the reader to reconsider a previously held position on the subject.

3. Reread the concluding paragraphs of the model essays and of the viewpoints in Section One. Which were most effective in driving their arguments home to the reader? What sorts of techniques did they use to do this? Did they appeal emotionally to the reader or bookend an idea or event referenced elsewhere in the essay?

4. Write a conclusion for the essay you have outlined and partially written in Exercise 1B using one of the techniques described above.

Exercise 3B: Using Quotations to Enliven Your Essay

No essay is complete without quotations. Get in the habit of using quotes to support at least some of the ideas in your essays. Quotes do not need to appear in every paragraph, but often enough so that the essay contains voices aside from your own. When you write, use quotations to accomplish the following:

- Provide expert advice that you are not necessarily in the position to know about
- Cite lively or passionate passages
- Include a particularly well-written point that gets to the heart of the matter

- Supply statistics or facts that have been derived from someone's research
- Deliver anecdotes that illustrate the point you are trying to make
- Express first-person testimony

Problem One
Reread the essays presented in all sections of this book and find at least one example of each of the above quotation types.

There are a couple of important things to remember when using quotations.

- Note your sources' qualifications and biases. This way your reader can identify the person you have quoted and can put their words in a context.
- Put any quoted material within proper quotation marks. Failing to attribute quotes to their authors constitutes plagiarism, which is when an author takes someone else's words or ideas and presents them as the author's own. Plagiarism is a serious infraction and must be avoided at all costs.

Write Your Own Persuasive Five-Paragraph Essay

Using the information from this book, write your own five-paragraph persuasive essay that deals with an aspect of Web 2.0. You can use the resources in this book for information about issues relating to this topic and how to structure this type of essay.

The following steps are suggestions on how to get started.

Step One: Choose your topic.
The first step is to decide on what topic to write your persuasive essay. Is there anything that particularly fascinates you about social networking and other Web 2.0 applications? Is there an aspect of the topic you strongly support or feel strongly against? Is there an issue you feel personally connected to or one that you would like to learn more about? Ask yourself such questions before selecting your essay topic. Refer to Appendix D: Sample Essay Topics if you need help selecting a topic.

Step Two: Write down questions and answers about the topic.
Before you begin writing, you will need to think carefully about what ideas your essay will contain. This is a process known as *brainstorming*. Brainstorming involves asking yourself questions and coming up with ideas to discuss in your essay. Possible questions that will help you with the brainstorming process include:
- Why is this topic important?
- Why should people be interested in this topic?
- How can I make this essay interesting to the reader?
- What question am I going to address in this paragraph or essay?
- What facts, ideas, or quotes can I use to support the answer to my question?

Questions especially for persuasive essays include:
- Is there something I want to convince my reader of?
- Is there a topic I want to advocate or oppose?

- Is there enough evidence to support my opinion?
- Do I want to make a call to action—motivate my readers to do something about a particular problem or event?

Step Three: Gather facts, ideas, and anecdotes related to your topic.

This book contains several places to find information about many issues relating to Web 2.0, including the viewpoints and the appendices. In addition, you may want to research the books, articles, and websites listed in Section Three, or do additional research in your local library. You can also conduct interviews if you know someone who has a compelling story that would fit well in your essay.

Step Four: Develop a workable thesis statement.

Use what you have written down in steps two and three to help you articulate the main point or argument you want to make in your essay. It should be expressed in a clear sentence and make an arguable or supportable point.

Example:

> **The open nature of the new Internet means that we all leave a trail, and we should be gravely concerned about this.**
>
> (This could be the thesis statement of a persuasive essay that argues that sites and applications that encourage users to post comments and reveal private information threaten privacy.)

Step Five: Write an outline or diagram.

1. Write the thesis statement at the top of the outline.
2. Write roman numerals I, II, and III on the left side of the page. Under each numeral write the letters A, B, and C.
3. Next to each roman numeral, write down the best ideas you came up with in step three. These should all directly relate to and support the thesis statement.
4. Next to each letter write down information that supports that particular idea.

Step Six: Write the three supporting paragraphs.
Use your outline to write the three supporting paragraphs. Write down the main idea of each paragraph in sentence form. Do the same thing for the supporting points of information. Each sentence should support the paragraph of the topic. Be sure you have relevant and interesting details, facts, and quotes. Use transitions when you move from idea to idea to keep the text fluid and smooth. Sometimes, although not always, paragraphs can include a concluding or summary sentence that restates the paragraph's argument.

Step Seven: Write the introduction and conclusion.
See Exercise 3A for information on writing introductions and conclusions.

Step Eight: Read and rewrite.
As you read, check your essay for the following:

- ✔ Does the essay maintain a consistent tone?
- ✔ Do all paragraphs reinforce your general thesis?
- ✔ Do all paragraphs flow from one to the other? Do you need to add transition words or phrases?
- ✔ Have you quoted from reliable, authoritative, and interesting sources?
- ✔ Is there a sense of progression throughout the essay?
- ✔ Does the essay get bogged down in too much detail or irrelevant material?
- ✔ Does your introduction grab the reader's attention?
- ✔ Does your conclusion reflect back on any previously discussed material and give the essay a sense of closure?
- ✔ Are there any spelling or grammatical errors?

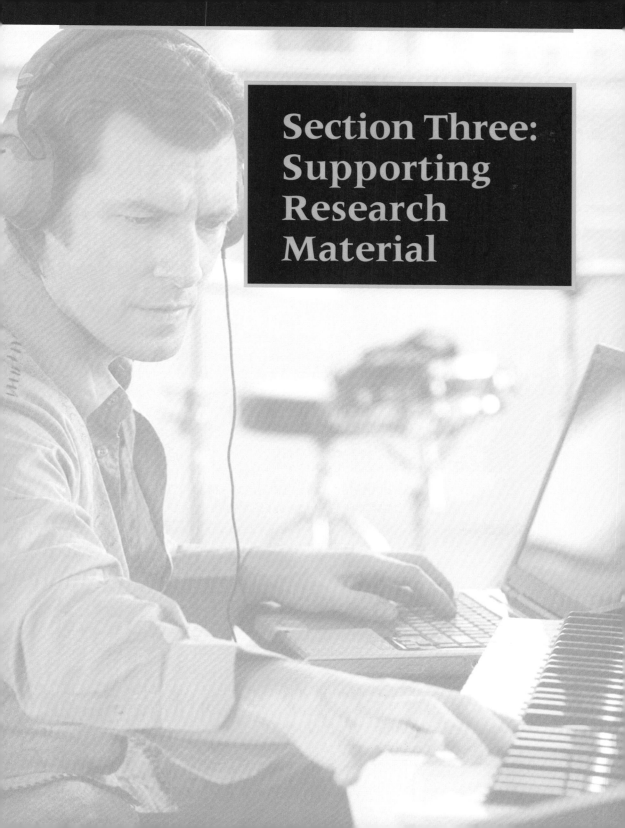

**Section Three:
Supporting
Research
Material**

Facts About Web 2.0

Editor's Note: These facts can be used in reports to reinforce or add credibility when making important points or claims.

The name "Web 2.0" was coined by American technology publisher Tim O'Reilly in 2004.

O'Reilly organized an Internet trade show and conference and reportedly brainstormed the name Web 2.0 Conference using the numbering convention of software updates. But O'Reilly did not mean there was a new version of the Web; he meant the Web was still important and offered interesting new opportunities. Disagreement over the definition of Web 2.0 continues; some call it "a meaningless marketing buzzword," others a radical change. (Oreilly.com, September 2005.)

Social Networking

A 2010 Pew Research Center survey found 47 percent of adults use social networking sites, compared with 73 percent of online American teens.

The first generation of social networks brought together strangers with a common interest:
- The WELL (founded by Larry Brilliant and Stewart Brand in 1985)
- Classmates.com (1995)
- Epinions (1999)

The second generation of social networks began by connecting users to people they already knew and/or chose to invite into their circle of friends:
- Friendster (founded by Jonathan Abrams in 2002)
- MySpace (2003)
- Facebook (founded by Mark Zuckerberg in 2004)

According to the British Broadcasting Company:

- Founded as a limited social network for college students, Facebook expanded membership to high school students in 2005 and anyone older than thirteen in 2006.
- In June 2010 Facebook logged 500 million active users.
- About 30 percent of these users are in the United States.

Facebook is free to users; its income comes from advertising. According to a May 2010 *Time* article, Facebook flashed more than 176 billion banner ads at users between January and March of 2010, more than any other site on the Internet.

In December 2009 Facebook released the first demographic study of its users. Among its findings:

- Between 2005 and 2009 the proportion of African American users rose from less than 7 percent to 11 percent.
- The proportion of Hispanic users rose from less than 4 percent to 9 percent.
- The proportion of Asian users fell from 8 percent to just over 6 percent.

According to a May 2010 survey by the Pew Research Center that showed diverging trends in social network users' concern for the privacy of their personal information:

- 71 percent of social networking site users aged eighteen to twenty-nine have changed the privacy settings on their profile to limit what they share with others online.
- At the same time, Internet users in general are less likely to express concern about the amount of information about them online: 33 percent said they worry about how much information is available about them, down from 40 percent in 2006.

Research by Oxford University professor of evolutionary anthropology Robin Dunbar contradicts the idea that users of social networking sites can maintain online relationships with hundreds or even thousands of people. Dunbar developed a theory in the 1990s that the human brain is capable of managing 150 friendships at most, a maximum unchanged throughout history. When Dunbar studied social networking sites to see if they stretched this limit, he found they did not: Users may like "friending" many hundreds of people, but actual traffic showed that users interact with the same inner circle of no more than 150 people on the Web, just like in the real world. (Chris Gourlay, "OMG: Brains Can't Handle All Our Facebook Friends," *Sunday Times* (London), January 24, 2010.)

Web Content

Since its founding in 2001, Creative Commons has issued licenses for more than 130 million works marked with the freedom their creators want them to carry, so others can legally copy, share, modify, or commercially use the content on the Web.

According to the Wikimedia Foundation:
- Wikipedia, created in January 2001, is one of the five most visited websites in the world.
- Wikipedia editions exist in more than 270 languages.
- Next to English (3.3 million articles), the largest editions are German (1.03 million articles), French (917,000 articles), Polish (677,000 articles), and Italian (661,000 articles).
- Wikipedia is continually expanded by roughly 100,000 active volunteer editors worldwide and has 364 million unique visitors per month.

Twenty-four hours of video are uploaded to YouTube every minute. (YouTube Fact Sheet, 2010.)

Twitter reports 6.2 new accounts per month, but about 40 percent of Twitter users have never sent a Tweet. (RJ Metrics, January 2010.)

Texting Habits

According to a December 2009 survey by the Pew Research Center's Internet & American Life Project:

- 4 percent of teenagers aged twelve to seventeen who owned cell phones said they have sent nude or nearly nude images or videos of themselves to someone else via text messaging, a practice dubbed "sexting."
- 15 percent said they have received sexting messages from someone they know.

A December 2008 survey by the National Campaign to Prevent Teen and Unplanned Pregnancy reported that 20 percent of teens had sent explicit images of themselves via cell phone.

According to a 2009 report by the Kaiser Family Foundation:

- Americans between the ages of eight and eighteen spend an average of seven and a half hours per day using some kind of electronic device (including computers, MP3 players, and cell phones).

In April 2010 the Pew Research Center reported that:

- half of Americans aged twelve to seventeen send at least fifty text messages a day, and
- two-thirds said they were more likely to use their phones to text their friends than to call them.

Blogging and Citizen Journalism

Participation and amateurism, two Web 2.0 principles, increase the need for Internet users to carefully evaluate Web pages for credibility and quality. A 2009 University of California, Berkeley guide includes the following indicators of high-quality information:

- Sources are documented with footnotes or links.
- The author and publisher of the information are clearly identified.
- A Google search of the author confirms that others think he or she is trustworthy.

An April 2009 *Wall Street Journal* article reports that more Americans now make their living as bloggers than as computer programmers or firefighters. Over 20 million Americans are bloggers, 452,000 of whom rely on blogging as their main source of income.

According to the Pew Research Center, the rise in bloggers and citizen journalists coincides with sharp declines in the number of journalists employed by major newspapers. For example, the seven Tribune Company papers (including the *Los Angeles Times* and the *Chicago Tribune*) employed a total of ninety-five journalists in their Washington, D.C., bureaus at their peak in the 1980s. By February 2009 those bureaus had merged into a single Tribune Company bureau, and the number of journalist was reduced to thirty-five.

A February 2010 study by the Pew Internet & American Life Project reports the following about social media and young adults:

- Blogging and blog commenting by teens and young adults has declined while blogging by adults has risen. Fourteen percent of teen Internet users say they blog, down from 28 percent in 2006.
- One-third of young adults post or read status updates on Twitter, compared with only 8 percent of teens.
- Ninety-three percent of Americans aged twelve to twenty-nine use the Internet. Among the core Internet activities of teenagers:
  - Sixty-two percent get news about current events and politics online.
  - Forty-eight percent buy books, clothing, or music online.
  - Thirty-one percent get information about health, dieting, or physical fitness online.
  - Seventeen percent turn to the Internet for information about topics that are difficult to discuss with others, such as drug use and sexual health.

Finding and Using Sources of Information

No matter what type of essay you are writing, it is necessary to find information to support your point of view. You can use sources such as books, magazine articles, newspaper articles, and online articles.

Using Books and Articles

You can find books and articles in a library by using the library's computer or catalog. If you are not sure how to use these resources, ask a librarian to help you. You can also use a computer to find many magazine articles and other articles written specifically for the Internet.

You are likely to find a lot more information than you can possibly use in your essay, so your first task is to narrow it down to what is likely to be most usable. Look at book and article titles. Look at book chapter titles, and examine the book's index to see if it contains information on the specific topic you want to write about. (For example, if you want to write about the effect of social media on Americans' lives and you find a book about the Internet in general, check the chapter titles and index to be sure it contains information relevant to your topic before you bother to check out the book.)

For a five-paragraph essay, you do not need a great deal of supporting information, so quickly try to narrow down your materials to a few good books and magazine or Internet articles. You do not need dozens. You might even find that one or two good books or articles contain all the information you need.

You probably do not have time to read an entire book, so find the chapters or sections that relate to your topic, and skim these. When you find useful information, copy it onto a note card or notebook. You should look for supporting facts, statistics, quotations, and examples.

Using the Internet

When you select your supporting information, it is important that you evaluate its source. This is especially important with information you find on the Internet. Because nearly anyone can put information on the Internet, there is as much bad information as good information to be found there. Before using Internet information—or any information—try to determine whether the source is reliable. Is the author or Internet site sponsored by a legitimate organization? Is it from a government source? Does the author have any special knowledge or training relating to the topic you are looking up? Does the article give any indication of where its information comes from?

Using Your Supporting Information

When you use supporting information from a book, article, interview, or other source, there are three important things to remember:

1. *Make it clear whether you are using a direct quotation or a paraphrase.* If you copy information directly from your source, you are quoting it. You must put quotation marks around the information and tell where the information comes from. If you put the information in your own words, you are paraphrasing it.

Here is an example of a using a quotation:

> Twitter has enjoyed such popularity because it is an easy yet satisfying way for people to jump on the social networking bandwagon. As one writer points out, "It requires a significant time commitment to actively participate in many of these trendy new forms of social media, like podcasting, blogging and video sharing; but Twitter just doesn't require that kind of effort, giving it the potential to be adopted by a broad niche of Web users who are looking for something more interactive than a MySpace profile but lower-maintenance than a blog." (McCarthy)

Here is an example of a brief paraphrase of the same passage:

> Twitter has enjoyed such popularity because it is an easy yet satisfying way for people to jump on the social networking bandwagon. Writer Caroline McCarthy points out that using most other forms of social media takes a lot of time and effort and requires someone to be comfortable using a computer. Twitter, on the other hand, is fast, easy, and nearly idiot-proof.

2. *Use the information fairly.* Be careful to use supporting information in the way the author intended it. Avoid taking information out of context or using evidence unfairly.

3. *Give credit where credit is due.* Giving credit is known as citing. You must use citations when you use someone else's information, although not every piece of supporting information needs a citation.

   - If the supporting information is general knowledge—that is, it can be found in many sources—you do not have to cite your source.
   - If you directly quote a source, you must cite it.
   - If you paraphrase information from a specific source, you must cite it. If you do not use citations where you should, you are *plagiarizing*—or stealing—someone else's work.

Citing Your Sources

There are a number of ways to cite your sources. Your teacher will probably want you to do it in one of three ways:

- Informal: As in the example in number 1 above, tell where you got the information as you present it in the text of your essay.
- Informal list: At the end of your essay, place an unnumbered list of all the sources you used. This tells the reader where, in general, your information came from.

- Formal: Use numbered footnotes or endnotes. Footnotes appear at the bottom of each page while endnotes are placed at the end of an article or essay, although they may be placed elsewhere, depending on your teacher's requirements.

Works Cited

McCarthy, Caroline. "In Defense of Twitter." CNET.com 30 May 2007. < http://news.cnet.com/In-defense-of-Twitter/2010-1038_3-6187323.html > .

Using MLA Style to Create a Works Cited List

You will probably need to create a list of works cited for your paper. These include materials that you quoted from, relied heavily on, or consulted to write your paper. There are several different ways to structure these references. The following examples are based on Modern Language Association (MLA) style, one of the major citation styles used by writers.

Book Entries

For most book entries you will need the author's name, the book's title, where it was published, what company published it, and the year it was published. This information is usually found on the inside of the book. Variations on book entries include the following:

A book by a single author:
> Axworthy, Michael. *A History of Iran: Empire of the Mind.* New York: Basic Books, 2008.

Two or more books by the same author:
> Pollan, Michael. *In Defense of Food: An Eater's Manifesto.* New York: Penguin, 2009.
> ———. *The Omnivore's Dilemma.* New York: Penguin, 2006.

A book by two or more authors:
> Ronald, Pamela C. and R.W. Adamchak. *Tomorrow's Table: Organic Farming, Genetics, and the Future of Food.* New York: Oxford University Press, 2008.

A book with an editor:
> Friedman, Lauri S., ed. *Introducing Issues with Opposing Viewpoints: War*. Detroit: Greenhaven, 2009.

Periodical and Newspaper Entries

Entries for sources found in periodicals and newspapers are cited a bit differently than books. For one, these sources usually have a title and a publication name. They also may have specific dates and page numbers. Unlike book entries, you do not need to list where newspapers or periodicals are published or what company publishes them.

An article from a periodical:
> Hannum, William H., Gerald E. Marsh, and George S. Stanford. "Smarter Use of Nuclear Waste," *Scientific American* Dec. 2005: 84–91.

An unsigned article from a periodical:
> "Chinese Disease? The Rapid Spread of Syphilis in China." *Global Agenda* 14 Jan. 2007.

An article from a newspaper:
> Weiss, Rick. "Can Food from Cloned Animals Be Called Organic?" *Washington Post* 29 Jan. 2008: A06.

Internet Sources

To document a source you found online, try to provide as much information on it as possible, including the author's name, the title of the document, date of publication or of last revision, the URL, and your date of access.

A Web source:
> De Seno, Tommy. "*Roe vs. Wade* and the Rights of the Father." The Fox Forum.com 22 Jan. 2009. < http://foxforum.blogs.foxnews.com/2009/01/22/deseno_roe_wade/ > Accessed May 20, 2009.

Your teacher will tell you exactly how information should be cited in your essay. Generally, the very least information needed is the original author's name and the name of the article or other publication.

Be sure you know exactly what information your teacher requires before you start looking for your supporting information so that you know what information to include with your notes.

Sample Essay Topics

The Benefits of Web 2.0 Outweigh the Risks

The Risks of Web 2.0 Outweigh the Benefits

Web 2.0 Is Killing Print and Television News

Web 2.0 Is Not to Blame for the Decline of Print and Television News

Interactivity and Amateurism Improve the Internet

Interactivity and Amateurism Degrade the Internet

Web 2.0 Degrades Politics

Web 2.0 Improves the Political Process

Hosts of User-Generated Content Are Responsible for Copyright Infringement

Hosts of User-Generated Content Are Not Responsible for Copyright Infringement

Online File Sharing Harms the Music Industry

Online File Sharing Does Not Harm the Music Industry

Social Networking Sites Expose Users to Scams, Cyberbullies, and Sexual Predators

The Dangers of Social Networking Sites Are Exaggerated

Virtual Communities Provide Valuable Social Interaction

Virtual Communities Keep Users from Developing Real-World Social Skills

Twitter Is a Useful Service

Twitter Is a Waste of Time

Sexting Should Be Illegal

Antisexting Laws Violate First Amendment Rights

Text Messages and E-mail Are Protected by the Fourth Amendment

Organizations to Contact

The editor has compiled the following list of organizations concerned with the issues debated in this book. The descriptions are derived from materials provided by the organizations. All have publications or information available for interested readers. The list was compiled on the date of publication of the present volume; the information provided here may change. Be aware that many organizations take several weeks or longer to respond to queries, so allow as much time as possible.

Berkman Center for Internet & Society
Harvard University, 23 Everett St., 2nd Fl.,
Cambridge, MA 02138 • (617) 495-7547
fax: (617) 495-7641 • e-mail: cyber@law.harvard.edu
website: http://cyber.law.harvard.edu

Founded in 1997, the center is dedicated to the study of the Internet and its effects on politics, law, and culture. Among its many projects are the OpenNet Initiative, which monitors and reports on Internet censorship and surveillance practices by governments, and Digital Natives, which studies the Internet use of a generation "born digital"—that is, young people who have been interacting with digital media all their lives. Publications include "Why Youth [Love] Social Network Sites," "A Tale of Two Blogospheres: Discursive Practices on the Left and Right," and "Media Re:public: News and Information as Digital Media Come of Age."

Center for Safe and Responsible Internet Use
474 W. Twenty-ninth Ave., Eugene, OR 97405
(541) 556-1145• e-mail: nwillard@csriu.org
website: www.cyberbully.org

The center was founded in 2002 by Nancy Willard, an authority on student Internet use management in schools and the author of *Cyberbullying and Cyberthreats: Responding to the Challenge of Online Social Aggression, Threats, and Distress.* In addition to briefs and guides for educators and parents, the center offers numerous reports, articles, and books for student researchers, including "Sexting and Youth: Achieving a Rational Approach," "Why Age and Identity Verification Will Not Work," and *Cyber-Safe Kids, Cyber-Savvy Teens.*

Consortium for School Networking (CoSN)

1025 Vermont Ave. NW, Ste. 1010, Washington, DC 20005
(202) 861-2676 • toll-free: (866) 267-8747
fax: (202) 393-2011 • website: www.cosn.org

Founded in 1992, CoSN is a professional organization that advocates and develops ways of using Internet technologies to improve teaching and learning in grades K–12. It supports the use of open-source software in schools to foster collaboration and allow teachers to modify and redistribute their applications. The center publishes the annual *Horizon Report* on emerging technologies and other reports, including "Web 2.0 in Education," which argues that schools must integrate social networking and participatory media or be left behind.

Creative Commons

171 Second St., Ste. 300, San Francisco, CA 94105
(415) 369-8480 • fax: (415) 278-9419
website: http://creativecommons.org

Creative Commons, a nonprofit organization founded in 2001, works to increase the amount of creative content (artistic, educational, and scientific) in "the commons"— that is, available to the public for free and legal use. It works alongside copyright, issuing free licenses to mark a work with the freedom the creator wants it to carry, so others can copy, share, remix, use commercially, or repurpose it. By 2008 more than 130 million works had been released under Creative Commons licenses on such well-known Web 2.0 platforms as Google, Flickr, PLoS, and Wikipedia. The Creative Commons website offers case studies and links to free works to illustrate the concept that free, Web-enabled use of intellectual property enhances creativity, innovation, research, and social life.

Electronic Privacy Information Center (EPIC)

1718 Connecticut Ave. NW, Ste. 200, Washington, DC 20009
(202) 483-1140 • fax: (202) 483-1248
website: http://epic.org

EPIC is a public interest research center founded in 1994 to raise public awareness of civil liberties issues related to emerging digital technologies and the Internet. It works to protect privacy and strengthen First Amendment rights; one example is its May 2010 complaint to the Federal Trade Commission that resulted in Facebook enhancing its privacy controls. EPIC publishes the online newsletter *EPIC Alert* and policy papers on topics such as medical records privacy, social networking, and government online surveillance. Other resources available at its website include a litigation docket of legislation on Internet privacy issues and an up-to-date archive of magazine and newspaper articles.

Federal Trade Commission (FTC)

Consumer Response Center, 600 Pennsylvania Ave. NW, Washington, DC 20580 • toll-free: (877) 382-4357
website: www.ftc.gov/bcp/menus/consumer/tech.shtm

The FTC, created in 1914, is the consumer protection agency of the federal government. It is officially responsible for investigating and prosecuting unfair and illegal business practices and identity theft on the Internet. Its Consumers & the Internet site explains user rights and risks regarding Internet access, commerce, computer privacy and security, spam, digital rights, and P2P file sharing. Website resources include numerous publications about the secure use of new digital technologies and a law-enforcement history of FTC Internet cases from 1994 to 2003.

Internet Education Foundation

Center for Democracy and Technology, 1634 Eye St. NW, Ste. 1100, Washington, DC 20006
(202) 638-4370 • fax: (202) 637-0968
e-mail: tim@neted.org • website: www.neted.org

Founded in 1996, the foundation is a nonprofit public interest group that works to educate and lobby policy makers and legislators in support of free expression and privacy in Web technologies. It supports the Federal Communications Commission's "net neutrality" proposals: government regulation of broadband providers to keep them from managing congestion on their networks in a discriminating way—for example, by favoring some kinds of transmissions or content over others. To keep providers from becoming gatekeepers, the foundation advocates narrow regulatory safeguards, not unlimited jurisdiction over the Internet. Position papers and conference proceedings are available on its website.

Internet Society (ISOC)

1775 Wiehle Ave., Ste. 201, Reston, VA 20190-5108
(703) 439-2120 • fax: (703) 326-9881
e-mail: isoc@isoc.org • website: www.isoc.org

The ISOC is an international, nonprofit organization founded in 1992 to help determine what global standards and policies should guide the growth of the Internet. Its goal is to increase the availability and utility of the Internet on the widest possible scale. It is a clearinghouse for Internet information and education and runs training programs for setting up Internet connections and enhancing digital literacy in developing countries. The society issues white papers and briefings on Web technologies and publishes a monthly online newsletter and the thrice-yearly *IETF*

Journal. Useful website resources include a history of the Internet, guidelines on the Internet code of conduct, and good descriptions of Internet infrastructure; for example, how the Web is organized, how IP and domain names are managed, and what bodies are responsible for operations and security.

National Middle School Association (NMSA)
4151 Executive Pkwy., Ste. 300, Westerville, OH 43081
(614) 895-4730 • toll-free: (800) 528-6672
fax: (614) 895-4750 • e-mail: info@nmsa.org
website: www.nmsa.org

The NMSA is an organization of some thirty thousand teachers, college students, parents, and community leaders interested in improving education for middle school students. The association publishes the monthly magazine *Middle Ground.* An especially useful resource is the February 2010 article "Tools for Schools: What's New with Web 2.0," which describes and provides links to more than twenty Web 2.0 tools for classroom use, including ThinkQuest, RSS feeds, the creative programming application Alice, Wordle, and Gabcast. This and many other publications are available on its website.

P2P Foundation
+ 31 20 772 8781 • e-mail: michelsub2004@gmail.com
websites: http://p2pfoundation.net/The_Foundation_for_P2P_Alternatives • http://blog.p2pfoundation.net/

Part wiki, part blog, part social network, the P2P (peer-to-peer) Foundation is a nonprofit, decentralized organization founded by Michael Bauwens in the Netherlands. It is dedicated to participatory culture: the concept of the Web as a worldwide community of users creating, collaborating on, and sharing free content, independent of advertising or government regulation. It is a clearinghouse of research on peer-to-peer practices and open-source content. Its extensive catalogs *Open Everything* and *Open Hardware Directory* link to content from complete operating systems such as

GNU/Linux to music and books to how-to building projects. As such, it serves as a messy, fascinating example of Web 2.0 in action.

Stanford Center for Internet and Society (CIS)

Stanford Law School, 559 Nathan Abbott Way, Stanford, CA 94305 • website: http://cyberlaw.stanford.edu

Founded in 2000, the center brings scholars, students, legislators, and programmers together to study the interaction of digital technologies and the law and how this interaction promotes or harms public goods such as free speech, privacy, intellectual property rights, diversity, and scientific research. It publishes the newsletter *Packets* about notable cyberlaw cases. Its Consumer Privacy Project wiki offers lists of free technologies to help Internet users gain better control over their data, such as anonymous surfing, plug-ins that reveal who is tracking a user online, and browser security improvements.

Wikimedia Foundation

149 New Montgomery St., 3rd Fl., San Francisco, CA 94105
(415) 839-6885 • fax: (415) 882-0495
e-mail: info@wikimedia.org
website: http://wikimediafoundation.org

The foundation is the parent organization of Wikipedia, its best-known project. It is a nonprofit charitable organization dedicated to developing and providing free, multilingual, educational Web content. Other projects (all collaboratively developed by users) include Wikimedia Commons, a collection of over 6.7 million free images, videos, and sound files; Wiktionary; Wikiquote; and Wikibooks. Its online press room offers press releases, statistics, and Q&As about the foundation's operations and philosophy.

Bibliography

Books

Bauerlein, Mark, *The Dumbest Generation: How the Digital Age Stupefies Young Americans and Jeopardizes Our Future (or, Don't Trust Anyone Under 30)*. New York: Tarcher, 2009.

Bonk, Curtis J., *The World Is Open: How Web Technology Is Revolutionizing Education*. San Francisco: Jossey-Bass, 2009.

Carr, Nicholas, *The Shallows: What the Internet Is Doing to Our Brains*. New York: Norton, 2010.

Dalby, Andrew, *The World and Wikipedia: How We Are Editing Reality*. Somerset, UK: Siduri, 2009.

Gillmor, Dan, *We the Media: Grassroots Journalism by the People, for the People*. Sebastopol, CA: O'Reilly Media, 2006.

Keen, Andrew, *The Cult of the Amateur: How Today's Internet Is Killing Our Culture*. New York: Broadway Business, 2007.

Powers, William, *Hamlet's BlackBerry: A Practical Philosophy for Building a Good Life in the Digital Age*. New York: HarperCollins, 2010.

Solove, Daniel, *The Future of Reputation: Gossip, Rumor, and Privacy on the Internet*. New Haven, CT: Yale University Press, 2008.

Tapscott, Don, and Anthony D. Williams, *Wikinomics: How Mass Collaboration Changes Everything*. Expanded ed. New York: Portfolio Hardcover, 2008.

Periodicals and Internet Sources

Anselmo, Anamaria, "Confessions of a Facebook Junkie," *Brown and White*, Lehigh University, January 30, 2009.

http://media.www.thebrownandwhite.com/media/stor-
age/paper1233/news/2009/01/30/Opinion/Confessions
.Of.A.Facebook.Junkie-3603597.shtml?refsource = college
headlines#5.

Banfield, Richard, "In Defense of Social Networking: A
Friend Is Still a Friend," *Mass High Tech: The Journal
of New England Technology*, May 15, 2009. www
.masshightech.com/stories/2009/05/11/newscolumn
1-In-defense-of-social-networking-A-friend-is-still-a-
friend.html.

Barras, Colin, "Innovation: How Social Networking Might
Change the World," *New Scientist*, February 27, 2009.
www.newscientist.com/article/dn16681-innovation-
how-social-networking-might-change-the-world.html.

Berton, Justin, "Are Lots of Teens 'Sexting'? Experts Doubt
It," *San Francisco Chronicle*, March 21, 2009. http://
articles.sfgate.com/2009-03-21/news/17214573_1_
sexual-health-cell-phone-sexting.

Brophy-Warren, Jameen, "The Good, the Bad, and the 'Web
2.0,'" *Wall Street Journal*, July 18, 2007. http://online
.wsj.com/article/SB118461274162567845.html.

Bunting, Madeleine, "Increasingly, the Rarest Experience
in Family Life Is Undivided Attention," *Guardian*
(Manchester), January 10, 2010. www.guardian.co
.uk/commentisfree/2010/jan/10/family-technology-
human-attributes-diminished.

Carr, Nicholas, "Is Google Making Us Stupid?" *Atlantic*,
July/August 2008. www.theatlantic.com/magazine/
archive/2008/07/is-google-making-us-stupid/6868/.

Chartier, David, "Future of Social Media: The Walls Come
Crumbling Down," *Wired*, June 2, 2009. www.wired
.com/dualperspectives/article/news/2009/06/dp_
social_media_ars.

Chaudhry, Lakshmi, "Mirror, Mirror on the Web," *Nation*,
January 29, 2007. www.thenation.com/article/mirror-
mirror-web.

Dautlich, Marc, and Nick Eziefula, "Web 2.0: New Internet, New Etiquette . . . New Law?" *Times Online* (London), October 23, 2007. http://business.times online.co.uk/tol/business/law/article2725636.ece.

Deresiewicz, William, "Faux Friendship," *Chronicle of Higher Education*, December 6, 2009. http://chronicle .com/article/Faux-Friendship/49308.

Dibbell, Julian, "Future of Social Media: Is a Tweet the New Size of a Thought?" *Wired*, June 2, 2009. www .wired.com/dualperspectives/article/news/2009/06/ dp_social_wired.

Dubner, Stephen J., "Is MySpace Good for Society? A Freakonomics Quorum," *New York Times*, February 15, 2008. http://freakonomics.blogs.nytimes .com/2008/02/15/is-myspace-good-for-society-a- freakonomics-quorum.

Fallows, James, "How to Save the News," *Atlantic*, June 2010. www.theatlantic.com/magazine/print/2010/04/ how-to-save-the-news/8095.

Fodeman, Doug, and Marje Monroe, "The Impact of Facebook on Our Students," National Association of Independent Schools, January 12, 2009. www.nais.org/ resources/article.cfm?ItemNumber = 151505.

Gillmor, Dan, "Journalism Isn't Dying, It's Reviving," *San Francisco Chronicle*, June 7, 2007. www.sfgate.com/ cgi-bin/article.cgi?file = %2Fchronicle%2Farchive%2F 2007%2F06%2F07%2FEDGGTP3FOE1.DTL.

Hogg, Chris, "Did the Internet Kill Journalism?" *Digital Journal*, May 11, 2009. www.digitaljournal.com/article/ 271696.

———, "Is There Credibility in Citizen Journalism?" *Digital Journal*, May 13, 2009. www.digitaljournal.com/ article/271657.

Holson, Laura M., "Breaking Up in a Digital Fishbowl," *New York Times*, January 6, 2010. www.nytimes .com/2010/01/07/fashion/07breakup.html?page wanted = all.

Kleinman, Zoe, "Children Who Use Technology Are 'Better Writers,'" BBC News, December 3, 2009. http://news.bbc.co.uk/2/hi/technology/8392653.stm.

Kornblum, Janet, "Meet My 5,000 New Best Pals," *USA Today*, September 20, 2006. www.usatoday.com/tech/news/2006-09-19-friending_x.htm.

Kroski, Ellyssa, "The Hype and the Hullabaloo of Web 2.0," Infotangle, January 13, 2006. http://infotangle.blogsome.com/2006/01/13/the-hype-and-the-hullabaloo-of-web-20.

McCarthy, Caroline, "In Defense of Twitter," CNET.com, May 30, 2007. http://news.cnet.com/In-defense-of-Twitter/2010-1038_3-6187323.html.

Northwestern University, "Student Facebook, MySpace Use Predicted by Race, Ethnicity, Education," *Science Daily*, November 22, 2007. www.sciencedaily.com/releases/2007/11/071119170137.htm.

Nussbaum, Emily, "Say Everything," *New York*, February 12, 2007. http://nymag.com/news/features/27341.

O'Reilly, Tim, "What Is Web 2.0? Design Patterns and Business Models for the Next Generation of Software," O'Reilly.com, September 30, 2005. http://oreilly.com/web2/archive/what-is-web-20.html.

O'Reilly, Tim, and John Battelle, "Web Squared: Web 2.0 Five Years On," paper delivered at the Web 2.0 Summit, San Francisco, October 20, 2009. www.web2summit.com/web2009/public/schedule/detail/10194.

Rosen, Christine, "Virtual Friendship and the New Narcissism," *New Atlantis*, Summer 2007. www.thenewatlantis.com/publications/virtual-friendship-and-the-new-narcissism.

Schwartz, Peter, "Facebook's Face Plant: The Poverty of Social Networks and the Death of Web 2.0," *Huffington Post*, December 9, 2008. www.huffingtonpost.com/peter-schwartz/facebooks-face-plant-the_b_149497.html.

Spencer, Jason, "Found in (My)Space," *American Journalism Review*, October/November 2007. www.ajr.org/Article .asp?id = 4405.

Stout, Hilary, "Antisocial Networking?" *New York Times*, April 30, 2010. www.nytimes.com/2010/05/02/ fashion/02BEST.html.

Sturm, James, "Life Without the Web," *Slate*, April–July 2010. www.slate.com/id/2249562/entry/2249563.

Sullivan, Bob, "Didn't You Know? Facebook Is Forever," Red Tape Chronicles, MSNBC.com, February 20, 2009. http://redtape.msnbc.com/2009/02/didnt-you-know .html.

Threshold, "Learning in a Participatory Culture," special issue, Spring 2009. www.ciconline.org/threshold-spring09.

Websites

Center for Citizen Media (http://citmedia.org/blog). Affiliated with the Walter Cronkite School of Journalism and Mass Communications at Arizona State University and the Berkman Center for Internet & Society at Harvard University, this site aims to enable and encourage grassroots media, especially citizen journalism. Articles and discussions focus on participatory journalism best practices, digital rights and fair use of Internet content, and search engine skills.

GetNetWise.org (www.getnetwise.org). The site is a public-service project of the Internet Education Foundation, a partnership of Internet industry corporations such as Google and Microsoft and nonprofit advocacy groups such as the Consortium for School Networking. It offers video tutorials and information related to online safety, spam, file-sharing, social networking, and privacy of information.

Pew Internet & American Life Project (www.pewinter net.org) This nonprofit "fact tank" conducts research and produces reports on the impact of the Internet on daily life, education, work and home, and civic and political life. The site offers updated, downloadable statistics on many topics, including Web 2.0, cloud computing, demographics, new media ecology, and the future of the Internet.

Index

Picture Credits

AP Images, 13, 32, 52
© Blend Images/Alamy, 39
© Eric Carr/Alamy, 37
Cengage/Gale, 14, 23, 31,40, 55
© Robert Christopher/Alamy, 17
© David J. Green—lifestyle themes/Alamy, 21
© Luxio/Alamy, 45
© NetPhotos/Alamy, 29
© RI screenshots/Alamy, 25
© Tetra Images/Alamy, 47

About the Editor

Lauri S. Friedman earned her bachelor's degree in religion and political science from Vassar College in Poughkeepsie, New York. Her studies there focused on political Islam. Friedman has worked as a nonfiction writer, a newspaper journalist, and an editor for more than ten years. She has extensive experience in both academic and professional settings.

Friedman is the founder of LSF Editorial, a writing and editing business in San Diego. She has edited and authored numerous publications for Greenhaven Press on controversial social issues such as Islam, genetically modified food, women's rights, school shootings, gay marriage, and Iraq. Every book in the *Writing the Critical Essay* series has been under her direction or editorship, and she has personally written more than twenty titles in the series. She was instrumental in the creation of the series and played a critical role in its conception and development.